Dominic R. Sondy

SAIGON SHUFFLE 2.0

Expanded Edition

Trish & Gary,
   This is sort of a beta edition
of my book (one of the first 20
printed). Joann and I have found
about a dozen errors, that we have
already corrected. Hope you enjoy
reading it anyway.....

[signature]

CREATIVE ACES PUBLISHING
CHICAGO, IL

DEDICATED TO ALL VETERANS

With special thanks to the
First Infantry Division and Joann Sondy

"What a long, strange trip it's been."

THE GRATEFUL DEAD

SAIGON SHUFFLE 2.0 EXPANDED EDITION

Published by Creative Aces Publishing, a division of Creative Aces Corporation; Chicago, Illinois

For information on discounts for bulk purchases, contact Creative Aces Publishing:
2144 N. Lincoln Park West 5B
Chicago, IL 60614
publishing@creativeaces.com
tel: 231-633-0945

ISBN-10:0984895051
ISBN-13:978-0-9848950-5-2

Book Design by Joann B. Sondy

*The unwilling, led by the unqualified,
doing the unnecessary, for the indifferent
and the ungrateful.*

ANONYMOUS

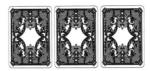

TABLE OF CONTENTS

TABLE OF CONTENTS

THE SHUFFLE

VIETNAM: *The place that proved we could be conned into war…*

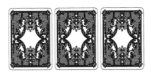

AUTHOR'S NOTE

By definition, all memoirs are written in hindsight. I will spare you the obvious cliché. This memoir begins like many other stories written about Vietnam. I was lucky to have survived. I was also fortunate to be able to serve in a capacity that allowed me to observe the war, as well as everyone involved, from multiple perspectives.

This memoir begins with some of my personal experiences as a combat infantryman. After all, this is a story about war. However, in Vietnam, there were as many as a dozen men in the rear supporting every combatant. Their stories are often overlooked so I've included some of those, as well. One of the most under-reported scenarios of all is that of the Vietnamese people. I have also noted some of the tragic consequences that played-out here at-home, after the war.

Please allow me to start at the beginning and tell you how I got involved…

PREFACE

There was a very real *existential risk* involved being a male living in the United States in 1968. All able-bodied young men were participants, willing or not, in a societal game of chance. The "game" was military conscription: **THE DRAFT**. Transforming the Draft into a lottery gave it the appearance of impartiality, provided camouflage for its sinister intent and trivialized the impact of being selected. It sounded so festive, anonymous numbers picked at regularly scheduled drawings. Aren't games supposed to be fun? How serious could it be? After all this was a *game*, what could go wrong?

George Orwell would have recognized the irony in the Draft's Lotto transformation. In a real lottery, people *choose* to play by buying tickets. In the Draft Lottery, young men were fined, or imprisoned, if they *didn't* play. In a real lottery, the *winning* number is selected. In the Draft Lottery *losers* had their number drawn. In a real lottery, the selected winner is *rewarded* with a valuable prize. Winning the Draft Lottery could *cost you* your life. *The Draft was not a lottery*.

The Draft was the opposite of a lottery; it was an anti-lottery. However, the Draft was still a "game" of chance. Military conscription was a game of chance; in the same way that Three Card Monte is a game of chance. In both scams, cards are shuffled and/or random numbers are chosen to promote the illusion of fairness, but the deck was stacked. In reality, human lives were randomly cast about like dice in some secret smoke filled back room. Living people were diminished; reduced to numbered pasteboards and dealt out. The Vietnam era Draft was a con game that deserved its own name: the *Saigon Shuffle*.

Poker players have a saying, *"Winners tell jokes. Losers say 'deal'."* The United States government was playing for high stakes and it was loosing. Like a compulsive gambler, the government's need was as unquenchable. They never told jokes. The U.S. government dealt its game from a huge stacked deck, which needed to be refreshed on a monthly basis. Unlike the NFL, many guys were drafted to play. Some were jinxed, were also dealt loosing hands and forced to cash-out way too early. Providence smiled on a very few. Ultimately, survival was just a case of being lucky.

The odds of drawing a helping hand (i.e. clerk, MP, truck driver, cook, mechanic, etc.), as opposed to the really bad deal of becoming a ground-pounding grunt, were never revealed. Just being in the game meant dangerous possibilities were close at hand. Yet, there had to have been some kind of statistic describing the ratio of Grunts compared to REMFs (Rear Echelon Mother Fuckers). There was considerable conjecture about the proportion of combatants to non-combatants, but those guesses were never verified. Some believed that there were as few as nine people supporting each infantryman. Other statistical suppliers placed the number at twelve support personal for every GI on the line. Either way, the Saigon Shuffle was about the luck of the draw. Of course, the government knew the odds. But, just like a casino, they weren't advertising how those odds were stacked against the participants.

The Saigon Shuffle was an international con game, devised by the United States. It was complex and involved many, mostly Asian, nations. The United States sponsored the Shuffle and sent invitations to China, Thailand, Laos, South Korea and even Australia. The people of Vietnam were coerced into hosting the Saigon Shuffle.

Hosting a war is <u>always</u> a losing proposition. With that single over-riding stipulation in mind, the population of Vietnam was **never** allowed to have a winning hand. The Saigon Shuffle was therefore, by rule, rigged against the Vietnamese people. The male citizens of Vietnam were the primary losers. However, the Saigon Shuffle's deck was deliberately stacked against all of the Vietnam's people. All able-bodied Vietnamese men were expected participate. Since this was a civil war, both sides insisted that male citizens had to serve–*or else*.

One way or another, *all* Vietnamese were destined to be exploited. The old, infirmed, women and children were ostensibly left out of their country's draft deal. But that didn't mean that they weren't involved or escaped risk. Being an innocent spectator in Vietnam

ANOTHER WAY OF LOOKING AT
THE SAIGON SHUFFLE

Besides being a strange con game, the *Shuffle* to Saigon could also be viewed as a dance step. Another definition of "shuffle" is a style of slow walking. So, the *Saigon Shuffle* could be thought of as a demented theatrical dance-step. Huge numbers of men were needed. Hundreds of thousands of young men (many involuntarily) lined-up, counted off, and *Hurried Up To Wait* so they could

perform their role in this ghastly production. The mostly male cast was choreographed and performed, gyrating to rock and roll, on a global stage. Their performance was staged, far away, in the Land of the Little People. So, the *Saigon Shuffle* was a long distance dance. The *Saigon Shuffle* had limited entertainment value and closed to bad reviews; its only applause came when it was finished. oo

PFC Dennis Kelly gettin' his grove on as he dances to the Saigon Shuffle.

provided no sanctuary. EVERYONE was randomly subjected to being shuffled around, sprayed with toxic chemicals, bombed, shot, killed or wounded.

As *spectators*, U.S. citizens were guaranteed safety, but even these observers paid dearly. The admission fee, for watching the carnage of the Saigon Shuffle, was paid in taxes and the blood of loved ones. All Americans had FREE access to live network coverage broadcast into their living rooms. Celebrated correspondents, with credentials dating back to WW II, provided color commentary as well as play-by-play descriptions. The horror of war was the nation's first "reality TV" regularly beamed into homes every evening. A lack of instant re-play distinguished the Saigon Shuffle from a sporting event and even that shortcoming was covered with updated multiple re-broadcasting. There was a running box score in the form of escalating numbers of dead and wounded. The score—body count—numbers were revised daily, even though the numbers were largely unverifiable and were probably bogus. The constantly increasing numbers were both surrealistic and unrealistic. Our team's players were being eliminated at an alarming rate. Of course the casualties were real people, not numbers. As the realization that the statistics were sons and relatives, the undeniable horror grew.

The Tet Offensive began January 30, 1968. The slaughter escalated. Tet lasted for only three weeks, but those three weeks never seemed to end. The death and destruction achieved new record levels. Many people died. North Vietnamese and Viet Cong forces took territory and eventually lost it. When the Tet Offensive was finally finished the invading North Vietnamese had gained no territory and sustained heavier losses than the South. Somehow this stunning defeat for the North was twisted into a loss for our side. It was more than a loss. It was a "pivotal" loss.

Walter Cronkite, a highly respected WWII journalist, declared that we had no chance of winning in Vietnam. Based on Mr. Cronkite's post Tet re-evaluation of the situation, many fans of the Saigon Shuffle became convinced that the war was 'unwinnable.' The "just" war was relabeled "endless quagmire." American spectators were booing. Defeat was snatched from the jaws of victory. Unfortunately, Mr. Cronkite, America's most trusted authority on war, had officially affirmed that victory was unattainable. Cronkite delivered his proclamation two weeks after I had volunteered for the draft.

Negative reviews, coupled with endless carnage, instilled declining enthusiasm. Nobody wanted to watch our team anymore. After ten seasons the Saigon Shuffle was finally canceled.

Somehow, inertia and backroom politics, kept the Saigon Shuffle going. The troops, and the Vietnamese people, didn't get the official memo about our loss until 1974. As Cronkite predicted, our team didn't win. It had to be someone's fault. Must have been the people we sent over to fight. After Tet, returning soldiers were no longer 'our boys.' Instead, warriors were labeled 'losers.' Unlike other warriors, soldiers returning from Vietnam had no homecoming. Some VFW posts wouldn't even accept Vietnam Veterans as members. Brave young men came home to jeers, some were even spit upon. They had done their best and were rewarded with disgrace and labeled "baby killers."

My narrative of the *Saigon Shuffle* begins just after the war's apex in 1968 and continues until 1986. The Vietnam War was never officially *declared* a war. It was just a *conflict*. Whatever it was, it officially ended in 1974. The consequences of the Saigon Shuffle con game reverberated through America for twelve years after the conclusion of hostilities. It took that long for the veterans to be repatriated, their blame renounced and their sacrifice acknowledged. A series of parades, through out the United Stated, in 1986, marked the Saigon Shuffle's finale and validated the veterans' patriotism. However, some people have never acknowledged the "wrongness" imposed upon Vietnam Veterans. Years after the conflict, I know people who continue to refer to me as a "baby killer."

RECRUITED (SUCKERED) INTO PLAYING THE GAME

My hometown, Roseville Michigan, is a working class suburb of Detroit. It is nestled between St. Clair Shores and Warren, just north of East Detroit. People living east of Woodward (the main street that runs from downtown Detroit north to Pontiac) refer to themselves as "Eastsiders." I am an Eastsider. I graduated from Roseville High School in June of 1965. Two-and-a-half years after graduation, I volunteered for the draft.

My timing was atrocious. How was I to know that the Tet Offensive (the turning point for the whole war) was going to be launched two months after I surrendered to the Macomb County Draft Board?

Perhaps I had done something extraordinarily stupid. I tossed the dice and played along with the government similar to the 1950s Groucho Marx game show, *You Bet Your Life*. It was also a move that I made to pay for my college education. Simply put, the United States Government would pay for school if I survived Vietnam. The odds favored the USA. My country had always won before. I would be able go to college for FREE and buy a house with no money down. How was I to know that everything changed? This was a totally different game. The prizes were the same, but this was the Saigon Shuffle. I thought I was tossing fate's dice, but the Saigon Shuffle was a card game, the same way that Three Card Monte is a card game. Anyone who thinks they can win at Three Card Monte is a sucker. Just like Three Card Monte, there were no winners in the Saigon Shuffle. Besides, in a way, I was coerced…

A combination of seemingly unrelated events compelled me to become involved in the Saigon Shuffle.

My parents had finally ended their relationship. They had successfully maintained a peaceful façade of their marriage for almost twenty-one years. Their charade crumbled and their partnership became history. As their oldest child, I had known that feelings of bitterness had been brewing beneath the surface of their marriage for a long time. By 1968, the role of "sacrificial victim" was the only thing that my mother and father shared. The state of their union was *unhappy*.

Each believed that *Parental Martyrdom*, in the form of enduring the torment of the other's company, was somehow validation their love of their offspring. Each partner claimed to have suffered, in a relationship of mutual loathing, for the **sake of the children**. Their children were no longer just *kids*—they transcended being mere 'offspring.' Each parent claimed to be a prisoner eternally chained to the other, bound by paternal responsibilities. As parents they had been forced to endure the horror of each other's company and those damned kids were somehow the foundation for their misery. There were cruel bonds that bound these two miserably unhappy mismatched people.

Mom and Dad's epiphany came with the realization that they didn't *have* to endure one another. Their misery didn't *have* to be endured, not for the sake of *anyone*; including their children. Mom finally made her contentions part of the public record. She filed, in the form of a divorce decree, at the Macomb County Courthouse.

For the duration of their extended conflict my parents had tried, individually, to recruit me into committing to either one's side or the other's. In the end, Dad simply let go of his end of the rope. However, the emotional tug-of-war didn't end with their divorce. Without Dad's pull, Mom's resolve stiffened. No longer having a meal ticket, Mom unilaterally appointed me, her oldest and only son, to be the person who would support her for the rest of her life. As far as my mother was concerned men were meal tickets. Because she had given me life, I obviously owed her. She had gone through the physical pain of having me as well as the emotional torment of living with my father because of me. I didn't just owe her—I owed her BIG time.

Until 1968, I had avoided participating in all disputes, foreign and domestic. My evasion of these situations was facilitated with an official, government sanctioned, *student deferment* and subsequent enrollment, at Central Michigan University (CMU).

I had applied to several universities. Quality of curriculum and academic reputations were marginal considerations. Location was my primary reason for choosing CMU. Central placed me furthest away from home and the local draft board. Going directly into the workplace (and/or even being only a "part-time" college student) had never been an option. That would have made me a candidate for another, even more menacing, kind of recruitment; the one offered by the government.

On the surface, my parents' struggle and the one in Southeast Asia were totally different. Surprisingly, both conflicts had some things in common. Both situations involved passionately divisive issues. Both conflicts shared a common time-line and had been escalating at about the same pace. Coincidently, for me, the nation's crisis and my parent's conflict arrived at a cusp simultaneously.

The United States government and my parents jointly wanted to make their problems become my problem.

Additionally, after three academically successful semesters at CMU, my savings and my father had both run out, simultaneously. To be fair, Dad didn't exactly *run* away. His departure, by his own account, could be more accurately described as having been *driven off*. Still, despite two full-time jobs, my money was gone. Financial support from my parents had been minimal before; now it was just plain non-existent. I returned home on the very same day that my father was leaving for the last time. Dad was anxious to hit the road. He didn't want to hear about my problems. We wished each other 'luck' in the driveway. Our parting handshake was sad and swift.

Mother, flushed with personal triumph, laid out her freshly revised agenda. She expected me to quit school, take a job at Ford Motor Company and support her. Her plan was simple, totally selfish, weird and kind of kinky. If Mother's scheme had involved death and sex it would have been Oedipal. Mom wasn't that cerebral.

Mom knew that my monetary options had become very *limited*. Dear mother simply wanted to use my deteriorating financial situation as leverage in her struggle to not have to work for a living.

After all, my mom had been a *homemaker* for most of her life and she wanted to remain a *homemaker*.

Mom never asked for my opinion and could have cared even less about my feelings. Now, with Dad history, Mom simply demanded my support. I had been blissfully excluded from the planning and execution of her divorce. Mother's predicament was her own creation. Yet, she expected me to be the solution for her new and unresolved problems.

Like Vietnam, Mom's plan had an element of long-term commitment with no clear exit strategy.

The Draft wasn't going away either. Friends pointed out that playing *You Bet Your Life* with the Army would qualify me for the GI Bill. I could go to college for *free*. All I had to do was take my chances and *survive*.

So, my choices were: (1) the Army (and Vietnam) or (2) living at *home* supporting my mother, my sisters and myself while working at Ford Motor Company *until the Army got me*.

Considering my mother's domestic strategy, the Tet Offensive seemed far away and the Army became an honorable solution that would allow me to avoid her problems.

THE DEAL

The prospect of being drafted hung, like the *Sword of Damocles*, over my head anyway. Might as well get it over with, I volunteered for the draft.

I had come from a long line of Army veterans. My grandfather had joined the Army, during World War I. His service helped to facilitate becoming an American citizen. Granddad's patriotism was rewarded with an encore trip back to Europe. His accommodations were muddy rat-infested trenches. He returned to the states as a freshly minted citizen with a brand new last name, 'Santa Maria' had become 'Sondy'.

My father had seen Europe, too. He fought the Germans in World War II. Maybe I would be fortunate enough to be the third generation to go to Europe at the government's expense? Not everyone went to Vietnam. Anyway, the service was temporary.

If I were lucky, my commitment would be finished in two years. If I wasn't so lucky, my obligation could terminate even sooner. Anything was better than staying home to play *momma's boy*.

My induction was scheduled for March 1968. I had 90 days to put affairs in order.

Yes, I was there for the iconic "The Who" performance.
Don't ask me what it was like...I don't remember.

Grande Ballroom playbills from March 1968.

THE UNWILLING

THE UNWILLING

After passing an abbreviated physical exam and swearing an oath of loyalty, I became a newly conscripted member of the United States Army. My first official order—line up in last name alphabetical order and count off by fours. We were divided into four groups using the same technique for making teams in gym class. It was so simple and familiar, but this was seriously different. This wasn't organizing teams of players into teams to play games. We weren't going to play anything. At this point, we weren't even people. We were raw material being processed. This was the beginning in a very long series of events that would determine my immediate future.

Our processing was something like cards being *shuffled* into the government's slots; pigeonholed by a seemingly random process that dictated our destiny. This time, providence had decided which branch of the military would benefit from our less-than-voluntary service. Apparently, luck plays a large part in influencing who would live and who would die. Those who were '1s' were sent into the Army, '2s' were going to serve as sailors in the Navy, '3s' would serve in the Air Force and the '4s' were going to become Marines.

Until that moment, I had thought that someone could only be drafted into the Army.

I was wrong about being drafted. Now, that I had seen why we had been ordered to count-off, I thought about how I might have stacked the deck for a more optimistic outcome. I could have served in the Air Force or Navy. I was relieved that I hadn't been chosen for the Marines.

The realization that I was involved in a "game" of chance meant there may be "rules" that could be manipulated. I began to consider the specific patterns that governed this unusual situation.

How could I work the rules to my advantage? Had I known, I could have moved one spot to my left and been in the Navy. I was going to have to pay more attention. It was important to learn more about the way this game was played.

It turned out that there was one *universal* rule for all branches of the military: *Hurry-up and Wait.* This unofficial mandate applies to the abstract concept of time. *Hurry-up and Wait* is similar to Zen meditation. The patience of a Buddhist monk is needed to acquire the specific level of understanding required to be enlightened enough to figure out what *Hurry-up and Wait* is about. *Hurry-up and Wait* is linked to contemplation because there's plenty of time, for thinking, while waiting.

The logic goes something like this: Everyone is expected to be on time. However, no event will ever be scheduled for the time when it will actually occur. Participants and attendees will always be scheduled to arrive early. The scheduling of anticipated wait time penalizes the early and on-time arrivals. Those who would have been considered late have to wait too because everyone is expected to hurry so they can wait. Eventually everyone arrives, and has waited, resulting in no one being late. This strangely twisted stoicism is essential to reach an understanding that many Eastern religions refer to as nirvana; in the Army it's just a normal state commonly known as SNAFU—*Situation Normal All Fucked Up.*

Fort Knox Kentucky was my fist duty station. Of course, we were required to hurry so we could wait for our flight.

Days were spent hurrying to be formed-up so we could:
- WAIT to be accounted for (multiple times daily),
- WAIT to be sorted,
- WAIT to measured–physically and intellectually,
- WAIT to be issued equipment,
- WAIT to be inoculated and
- WAIT to line-up, *and*
- WAIT some more.

Recruits had their hair sheared off, were tested, vaccinated, and lectured. All of these things took time and much of that time was spent waiting. We were less than meat being processed; we were just numbered cards, endlessly shuffled, made to wait and eventually dealt.

Individuality was deliberately synthesized away and replaced by more easily shuffled anonymous numbers. Everyone was assigned a number. That number, along with blood type and religious preference, was embossed onto metal dog tags and hung on a chain around our necks. Each service number had a prefix: US meant Unvoluntary Service (draftee), RA designated Regular Army (volunteer), NG National Guard, O for Officer.

Our future jobs would also be described in a numbered code: we would have a 'Military

The official photo that would have been sent to my hometown newspaper, *if...*

Occupational Specialty' (or MOS). Pay grades were an even simpler number system.

There were over two hundred men in my basic training company, which was divided into platoons and assigned to four wooden barracks. The barracks were built during World War II. The area in front of the buildings was referred to as the Company Street. We assembled (formed-up) on the Company Street and went everywhere as a group. Three semesters of college ROTC meant that I was qualified to become a Basic Training squad leader.

Since we were in Basic Training, we didn't have access to television or newspapers. Martin Luther King Jr. was assassinated on April 4, 1968. The news of his death was accompanied by a rumor that civil unrest was almost certain. The residents of my home town, Detroit, had rioted and burned the city less than a year before. The National Guard had been called in to stop that insurrection. There was already a certain level of apprehension involved in being a member of the Army. The recent Tet Offensive in Vietnam had already notched-up everyone's sense of foreboding. The added uncertainty of civil disorder, heightened by the assassination of Dr. King, inflated the tension even more.

Then things got really bad.

At the end of Basic, I drew about the worse assignment anyone could draw. I was going to Tigerland, Fort Polk Louisiana. My new duty assignment would mean two summer months in the humid heat of the most bug-infested post in the United States. I would be training to become a Light Weapons Infantry Specialist (11B10). The odds of *not* fighting in Vietnam were narrowed to *non-existent*. The only thing that could make such a lousy draw of the cards even worse would have been going directly to Louisiana with no leave or time off. That happened, too. No one going into the infantry was allowed leave, not even a weekend pass. My orders were to go directly for the stinking swamps. *Do not pass goal do not collect $200*. At least I wouldn't be going to Fort Polk alone, about half of the guys in my Basic training company were going with me.

There was a graduation ceremony. After commencement, we were ordered to jam all of our new military belongs into our new duffle bags, line-up in the company street and wait for transportation that would take us past the United States [Gold] Bullion Depository at Fort Knox, one last time, and back to the airport. My second airline adventure ended at an Air Force Base in Texas then we were bused to Louisiana.

Company commanders are traditionally Captains. Ours was a First Lieutenant, his last name was Lewis. Lt. Lewis had just returned from a tour in Vietnam and was planning to leave the Army at the end of our training cycle.

Lieutenant Lewis explained that he was going to do his best to teach us everything that we would need to know. We were going to learn everything essential for surviving our inevitable yearlong Vietnam tour in the 'Land of the Little People'. This knowledge would be jammed into an eight-week course. He didn't sugar coat it. Life was going to be hard. All of us were going to Vietnam. Some of us would not be coming back. We were going to become proficient in self-defense while we simultaneously developing the offensive skills required to eliminate our enemy. Everyone was going to learn to shoot and maintain, M-16's, as well as various machine guns. We would fire rocket and grenade launchers. Throwing real live old-fashioned hand grenades was part of the training, too. Some attention would be paid to first aid and tending to the horrible wounds that some of us were sure to receive. Everyone would become even tougher than we already were. Only the tough would survive.

I'm not exactly sure why Lt. Lewis signed-on for me to have a secondary MOS. I wasn't able to ask him, because I didn't know that my CO had authorized the unusual additional skill proficiency, until advanced training was over, and Lt. Lewis and I had gone our separate ways. I didn't know about the impact Lt. Lewis' impetuous decision would have on my fate. It took four months to discover how Lewis influenced my fate

I learned of Lt. Lewis' generosity on my last day at Fort Polk while I read the *otherwise* boring folder that contained my service records. Actually, I was killing time, hurrying-up to wait, on my way to my next assignment.

Lieutenant Lewis was probably 'hurrying-up-to wait' while he was on his way to becoming a civilian, again. I was on my way to a surprise Non-commissioned Officer's School appointment at Fort Benning Georgia. This assignment was surprising because NCO School was voluntary duty that I hadn't volunteered for. My secondary MOS as a photographer was even more surprising because it may have had something to do with a *smart-ass* remark I made during a barracks inspection.

Back in basic training, I had been an intern-squad leader, I shared a room with four other squad leaders and a recruit-platoon leader. Our area was not inspected as thoroughly, or as often, as the rest of the barracks. Here, in Advanced Training, I was just another buck private with a bottom bunk in the downstairs area of the barracks.

I stood at attention, like everyone else, staring into the aisle waiting to be inspected. My vertical locker door was open behind me and my footlocker laid open at my feet. We were allowed to post pictures on the inside door of our vertical locker. Most guys had pictures of their families and girlfriends. I, too, had a photograph of a girl, who was no longer my girlfriend. Jeri had dumped me when I announced that I had volunteered for the draft. Apparently she didn't want to wait for my return. I believe, she enjoyed the sadistic pleasure watching my reaction while she dumped me in person as opposed to the anonymity of a "Dear John" letter. Still, a rather attractive photograph of her was taped inside my vertical locker door. I had taken the color picture. I was proud of my work, as well as her appearance and had the picture printed as an 8x10.

Even though my photographic subject no longer cared if I lived or died, I was proud of the nice picture of a pretty girl that I had taken. This particular picture featured Jeri wearing a jacket and tight jeans in a reclining pose on a frozen Lake St. Clair. She was laying on her side with her very attractive upper body propped-up on one elbow. The image was taped, at eye-level, on my locker door. It was stifling hot in the barracks. Jeri was a very cool blonde. Lt. Lewis approached as I stared into the empty aisle behind him. The Platoon Sergeant accompanied him with a clipboard, his pencil positioned for instant demerits. Lieutenant Lewis asked, "Where did you get that picture of that nice looking girl?"

"Sir, I shot it, Sir." I proudly replied, with the straight-faced seriousness that is required during a military inspection.

Apparently the Lieutenant wanted to have some fun with the solemn recruit standing stiffly before him. "Is she your girlfriend Private?" he asked.

"Sir, she was before the Army got me, Sir." I answered.

Lieutenant Lewis' grin widened as he asked, "She give good head Private?"

"Sir, I don't think that's any of your business, Sir." I responded instantly, without a beat of hesitation.

I was still focused on the empty aisle. But, on the edge of my vision I could see the Platoon Sergeant roll his eyes. Lt. Lewis wasn't smiling. He spun on his heels.

Rebuffed, my Commanding Officer was already on his way to inspect the next private. I didn't get a demerit. Thank you, former First Lieutenant Lewis, where ever you are! Instead, I discovered that I had been granted a very rare secondary MOS 71Q20, as a photographer, along with my promotion in rank to Private First Class (PFC).

LED BY THE UNQUALIFIED

It isn't that they couldn't see the solution.
It's that they couldn't see the problem.

GILBERT KEITH

TERRY WISE

Along with the additional MOS, I had received those surprising orders to report to Fort Benning's NCO school. No leave time, just get on the plane. I liked Lt. Lewis, as my company Commanding Officer, he razzed me. After than inspection, Lewis would give me shit. In a jocular kind of way he got back his authority by sort of picking on me. He was never mean spirited. We shared a kind of good-natured banter like a teacher might have with a class clown.

My initial reaction to this involuntary assignment was that it was some sort practical joke–*a parting shot*. After I thought about it, my CO probably had some quota to fill. He probably thought, "Somebody's got to go, why not send the smart-ass?" Again, I was not the only one to receive orders for a voluntary school that I hadn't volunteered.

"But NCO school is *voluntary*." I explained to Terry Wise. "The only reason they're sending us to NCO school is because they need more sergeants. Sergeants are dropping like flies. They are getting killed faster than new ones can be promoted. The Army considers people to be replaceable assets. When some equipment is needed, they requisition more and send it where it is called for. We're not much different than military property. The Army needs more sergeants, they just requisition more and send them where they're needed. You and I are just replacing the broken ones that they sent home in a box."

Terry was also on his way to NCO school. Our military experience began at the same time, we had gone through both Basic Training and Light Weapons Infantry Training in the same training companies. Terry and I hadn't met until we were given some break time (in the form of a weekend pass) at Fort Polk. It was the first weekend pass I had received since being inducted into the Army over four months ago.

Originally, I had wanted to use my first week-end pass to go to New Orleans 150 miles away. There was no civilian airport where I could catch a flight. A Greyhound bus trip would have taken almost 12 hours–*each way*–and would have killed most of my limited pass time. Hitchhiking was ruled-out because the red-neck civilians living in Louisiana had a reputation of being inhospitable toward strangers (remember what happened to the guys in the movie *Easy Rider*?). So, Terry and I settled for exploring the souvenir shops and bars in Leesville. Terry was a draftee from Louisville, Kentucky.

"But, it's a *voluntary* school," I continued. "I don't think that I want to wear a target in the form of Sergeant chevrons. Besides, I did not volunteer."

"I didn't volunteer either," Terry said. "But we'll get more pay and never get stuck with KP."

"Remember, back at the beginning of Basic, when they offered everybody a chance to become a Warrant Officer? The Army needed people to fly helicopters. It was the same kind of deal. Pilots are getting killed faster than they can train new ones. They were even willing to let guys who wear glasses become pilots. There was a catch, back then. I'll bet that we will have to sign-up for more time in the service; just like the Warrant Officer Flight School volunteers. Sure, we'll get better pay. But we'll also get a much better chance of being killed; just like Warrant Officer Flight School training.

I don't know about you, but my goal is to survive and get honorably discharged. I'm not looking for a career. I just want to get on with my life without the draft hanging over my head." I said.

Terry and I continued our debate, about the voluntary school we hadn't volunteered for, as we flew to Atlanta plus the bus that took us to Columbus, Georgia. We had plenty of time to consider our situation and weigh our options.

NCO School, or no NCO School, Terry and I had been in the Army since March, neither of us had any leave time-off. We weren't able to ask for the advice of friends back home. So, we became friends and figured it out for ourselves. By the time we arrived at the NCO training center we had convinced ourselves that becoming sergeants was not a good thing.

The welcoming speech was given in a big auditorium filled with hundreds of Non-commissioned Officer candidates. Terry and I were seated in the middle of the front quarter of the large crowd. Our new potential Commanding Officer addressed the multitude from a podium on the elevated stage. He enthusiastically explained how lucky everyone in the audience really was, *we were the chosen elite*. We had been selected because we were the *best of the best*. All of those in attendance were the *crème de la crème*; *carefully* handpicked volunteers destined to become leaders of men. We all shared the great honor to have been nominated, "…and any damn coward who hasn't the guts to face-up to the hard work and trials that we are certain to face in the coming weeks should stand-up and leave right NOW!"

I looked at Terry. Terry looked at me. The speaker may have been making a rhetorical statement; but we couldn't have asked for a better exit line. We didn't say a word, just stood (in unison), made our way to the aisle and headed for the back of the room.

The entire hall waited and watched, in absolute silence as we made our way to the back. It was like we were in a slow motion movie. Eventually, we found ourselves in a large vestibule by the entrance. We almost broke into nervous laughter. We had done it! But we weren't finished yet. Time seemed to drag on forever, as we waited in the quiet of that lobby, for the consequences that were sure to come.

"We're going to have some explaining to do." I said in a voice that was almost a whisper. We hadn't planned for what would happen next. Maybe we didn't believe that we would actually walkout. We didn't have any idea about our next move. We just knew that we didn't want to be milling around in the lobby when the ceremonies were over and hundreds of enthusiastic non-commission-officer candidates came pouring through the swinging doors we had just so nonchalantly strolled through. Would we be trampled in a stampede? Maybe we would be dragged outside and become the subject of public ridicule?

None of that happened.

Some Sergeant came over to us and sent us on our way.

Terry and I were put in a cab and taken back to the company area where our duffle bags had been stowed. The cab waited for us and eventually brought us to our next destination—another Training Company.

We were among the first arrivals for another training cycle. This group of NCO candidates was scheduled to start in two days. For a couple of hours, Terry and I had an entire barracks all to ourselves. These barracks were "nicer" than those we had been assigned to at Ft. Knox or Ft. Polk. The buildings looked the same on the outside, but inside the barracks were divided into cozy smaller rooms. Each room was designed to accommodate two trainees with a bunk and two sets of lockers. The room featured a central study table, two chairs and two desk lamps. We picked a cubical close to the door. Our alibi, for the arriving candidates, was that we were "overflow" from a different training cycle, that started yesterday, our new orders hadn't caught-up with us yet.

The next day Terry and I were bused, along with a couple of training companies of cadets, to another huge assembly hall. This time, when everyone was asked to be seated, we hung-back, waited and found two seats in a back row right on the aisle. The presentation was amazingly similar to the last performance we had attended. Everyone in the audience was declared to be *lucky, elite, best of the best* and *honored*. A totally different officer touched all of the exact same points, using identical clichés, in almost exactly the same order! Terry and I waited for our cue. This officer delivered our exit line with a level of enthusiasm that matched the last orator.

The speech wasn't the only thing that seemed like *déjà vu*. The cab ride to another training cycle was the same and the dorm room barracks were similar (except this place actually had curtains on the windows!). This training company's point of exceptionalism was its mess hall. This company's cook must have been a chef in civilian life.

He served the best breakfast peach fritters, with hot maple syrup, that I have ever tasted.

For two weeks, Terry and I were bounced from one cycle to another. The escalating amenities reached a plateau after the best mess hall. Being bumped from one training company to another had become formulaic. Terry and I habitually positioned ourselves in the back of auditoriums. The introductory ceremonies became so familiar that we had inadvertently memorized the welcome speech. We waited, never anticipating, for our cue to be delivered before leaving quietly. We believed that courtesy was *de rigueur* and it would have been rude to leave before our exit line was delivered. We agreed that "… can leave NOW" was an invitation that we had to accept. Without that prompt we might not have made our discreet move toward the door and may have inadvertently become sergeants. Sometimes we would quietly critique a presenting officer's delivery while we waited in the vestibule for our ride. Our initial fear of the unknown had been replaced by the over-confidence of routine. For a short time, it appeared that Terry and I would spend the remainder of our Army careers living between training cycles.

The illusion of security vanished when a kindly older Major ambushed us in the lobby of what turned out to be our last assembly hall. He was the man who wanted to hear our excuse. We had been expecting him since that first welcome reception. This Major wanted to hear that explanation I had expected to be asked for way back when we had walked out of that very first training cycle two weeks before. The moment of truth had finally arrived.

Mark Twain once said, "You don't have to remember anything if you tell the truth." So, I just spit it out:

> *"Sir, Wise and I don't mind serving our country. We're not conscientious objectors or anything like that. But when we were drafted, we figured that we would serve our two years of active duty and get back to our civilian lives. Sir, neither of us volunteered for NCO School."*

Terry was compelled to throw in his two-cents worth, "Sir, Sondy's right about our not volunteering. We're not trying to make waves or anything. I really have a problem with signing on for the extra time we would have to be in the Army. And NCO School just doesn't add-up.

"If we were to go through with this training, and did a tour in Vietnam, our time would add up to more than the two years that we were drafted. At some point, someone is going to have to ask us to extend our time in the service. Sir, if I had wanted to do that, I would have just enlisted in the first place. If I had enlisted I might have had a choice about Advanced Training schools. But I didn't enlist and I didn't volunteer for NCO School."

OK, we told the Major *half* of the truth. Neither of us wanted to explain our theory about the Army's motivation for having the NCO School in the first place. Going into the weeds complaining about the mortality rate of sergeants in Vietnam could lead to an argument over the logic behind our reasoning. Even a Private First Class knows that he can't win an argument with an officer. So Terry and I had agreed, in advance, that we would keep our explanation brief, on point and not make it look like the guys who did go to NCO School were easily manipulated or idiots. After all, when selling someone (even a Major) an idea, knowing when to stop talking is important.

The Major listened to us and reflected upon our concerns. He kept us in suspense as he considered our immediate future. "You boys know that you will be getting orders to go to Vietnam?"

"Sir, we've been expecting those orders from the moment we were sent to Fort Polk."

"OK. I'll send you to a casual company. They'll find something to keep you busy while you wait for your new orders. It could take as long as six weeks." He shook our hands and wished us luck.

Fort Benning was one giant training center. Non-Commissioned Officers, Officer Candidates, Air Borne trainees even Army Rangers and Green Berets all had schools there. The washouts, from all these schools, were assigned to various casual companies to wait for new orders.

A big empty parade ground separated our casual company from the huge amusement park structures used by the Air Borne trainees. Towering iron derricks, topped with several long booms, were fitted with cables that hoisted soldiers, dangling from parachutes, high into the air. The trainees were eventually released to float gently back to earth where they would run around until they could be hoisted back-up again. Air Borne was a two-week school. It looked like fun, compared to the swamps back at Ft. Polk. The only catch: Air Borne trainees ran *everywhere*. I pictured them running, in place, while they used the latrine.

Officer Candidates also ran everywhere. Future second lieutenants automatically became sergeants (until they graduated) and had FOLLOW ME insignia sewn onto their fatigues.

Everyone in a Casual Company is a transient awaiting orders to go somewhere. The temporarily displaced were called into a morning formation and given assignments for the day. The tasks were the usual Army busy work: cleaning barracks in preparation for a new training cycle, picking-up trash, working in the mess hall doing KP or *my favorite* painting rocks. Our evenings were always free for catching a movie, going to the PX or hanging-out somewhere drinking 3.2 beers. There were no work formations called on the weekends. So Friday or Saturday evenings could be spent, just over the Georgia state line, in Phenix City, Alabama.

Terry and I had spent a Saturday evening or two off-base in Leesville, just outside Fort Polk. Leesville had a brightly lit area at one end of Main Street, relegated to GIs. The blocks-long strip was lined with souvenir stands, pawnshops and places selling deep-fried salty foods along with ice-cold beer. The Big Casino was Leesville's real main attraction. A short walk down a near-pitch-dark cockroach infested side street lead to Leesville's legendary bar/whorehouse.

What the Big Casino lacked in décor it compensated for by its size, it was a mammoth pole barn. A mostly deserted gravel parking lot accented the front of a looming sheet metal building. The whole structure was made from corrugated metal and shared its dimensions with my high school gymnasium. Like my high school gym, it had its own special sweaty smell. The dark interior of the Big Casino had an additional special earthy musk aroma. The overall reek contained the combined essence of tobacco smoke, stale beer and urine. It was too dark inside to make out color on the walls, if there was any. Swirling spots of colored lights, reflected from a clichéd rotating mirrored disco-ball suspended in the high ceiling, offered moving glimpses of a cluster of empty tables and chairs. The big hardened earth dance floor was also empty. A glowing jukebox supplied the cavernous space with most of its light as well as some scratchy Patsy Kline. A long stool lined bar occupied one wall. Hookers were stationed among the bar stools. The ladies plied their trade in a series of trailers scattered outside, behind the looming building. Even with due consideration afforded to Leesville's service-based charm; Leesville was little more than a small-town carnival.

Phenix City Alabama was the genuine Big Top–a bona fide three-ring circus. Both towns were accessed, from their respective military bases, by regularly scheduled yellow school bus shuttles. Both towns had similar bars, greasy food, souvenir shops, tattoo parlors and pawnbrokers. Phenix City was much larger than Leesville. Phenix City supported way more than one rustic whorehouse. It was a much more happening place than Leesville. Phenix City had a wider assortment of mischief available until the wee hours.

Since the wussy yellow school bus shuttle only offered limited hours of transportation, many of the heartier military celebrants deferred to the not-so-gentle hospitality of the Fort Benning Military Police for their return ride. The MPs provided a fall back lift back to base in their own very special *olive drab limo.*

The MP's green limo was usually centrally parked, just off of Phenix City's hyperbolized main street. This alternative ride featured utilitarian wooden benches mounted inside a heavy wire cage welded onto the back of an Army duce and a half. The limo's single door could not be opened from the inside. Since the entire passenger compartment, including its roof, was composed of continuous wire-mesh there was no shelter from rain. Despite the ample ventilation and the random rain-water flush, the green limo managed to stink with a stench that was unique to the *bouquet* produced by a combination of sour vomit, used beer and rancid fry grease. Neither Terry nor I had the honor of being chauffeured in the limo, but anyone walking within twenty feet of that vehicle could attest to its unforgettable fragrance.

Phenix City surpassed Leesville in one other important category: Phenix City was considerably more violent than Leesville–*or just about anywhere else on earth.* Walking down the street on a hot and sticky humid summer evening, Terry and I could chose between watching a drunken brawl, witnessing a mugging, or seeing someone having their teeth kicked out on the street's curb. Show times, actors, and performance times varied with every passing block. Open bar room doors gushed blaring renditions of Creedence Clearwater Revival's *Fortunate Son*. Creedence provided the perfect musical background for the surreal sights, smells and action. Remaining a spectator, as opposed to becoming an unwilling participant, was always a tricky priority. There were no rules, no local police and not nearly enough MPs.

Back on base, Terry spent less than a week working at those mundane Casual Company chores. Instead, he found a totally unorthodox gig. Terry tried-out, and became, an infielder on an intramural baseball team. Every morning, after formation, he was shuttled off to baseball practice. Always thinking outside the box, Terry told me about another special job he had seen posted on the bulletin board outside the orderly room. He thought this particular posting would be perfect for me. The Fort Benning Photo Lab needed a technician. Brandishing the orders that established my secondary MOS photographic skills, I applied for this unique position. My credentials were accepted. Every morning, after formation, I was taken *by cab* to my new job making prints at the air-conditioned laboratory.

Civilians staffed the lab. Since I was the only GI working there, no one had the authority to order me to do anything. Technically, I could have just shown-up and loafed all day. But someone would have noticed, eventually, and I really didn't want to go back to Casual Company busy work. Besides, these were nice people. I wanted to help. So, I hung-out at the lab and made pictures every weekday while waiting for the orders that would send me to Vietnam.

The inevitability of the fall approaching was signaled by shorter days. The countdown to Vietnam was as inescapable as the change of the seasons. Terry and I received our orders to report to Fort Dix New Jersey.

Our date with destiny had been set—WEDNESDAY, OCTOBER 9, 1968. After identical 30-day leaves, the 'Wise' man and I would meet-up at Fort Dix and probably leave on the same plane.

My much-anticipated thirty-day vacation turned out to be an anticlimactic letdown. The sadness of returning home, for what could have been the last time was almost disappointing. At first, all my friends and family were glad to see me. But, after a very short time, it became obvious that everyone had jobs and other things to do. The novelty of visiting wore off; boredom and self-pity set in. "Was this going to be the last time we would see each other?" began to weigh heavily on every person I saw.

I was only twenty years old. The drinking age was 21. Up until that point I had not really even tried to drink in a bar in Michigan. Then it occurred to me: *Why Not Live It UP?* No judge is going to throw me in jail. What was the worst thing that could happen? Would they send me off to Vietnam? What did I have to loose?

Finding a bar where I could watch the World Series became my personal objective for the final weeks of my leave. Being drunk was fitting, harmless and *fun*. Finding a partner to accompany me on this adventure didn't very take long. Gordie, a good friend since junior high, was already twenty one. Since Gordie was already old enough to drink legally, I was only thrown out of two or three places before we found acceptance.

It was the perfect spot: a topless bar on Eight Mile Road. It featured a runway length stage that was centered in a rectangular room. The bar, and barstools, completely surrounded the stage with tables chairs lining the walls. Chairs, instead of booths, afforded patrons a clear view of the television mounted on the back wall. The lunch crowd had left the bar nearly empty when Gordie and I found a seat near the TV. This was the place where we whiled away the last afternoons of my only leave. Getting drunk, watching the 1968 World Series in the company of scantily clad girls was the way I will always remember my only military leave. Gordie and I even visited that bar when the Tigers *weren't* playing. Every day, for almost two weeks, we became regular bar patrons. The dancers and bartenders knew, and greeted us. A good time was had by all.

The first two World Series games were played away, in St. Louis. The Tigers lost the first game 4-0. They came back to beat the Cardinals 8-1 in game two. Detroit lost games three and four, at home, with scores 7-3 and 10-1. They were down, in the series, with three loses and only one win. The Tigers managed to pull out a 5-3 win in their last home game of the series. The 1968 World Series was far from even when the Detroit Tigers and I left town. The Tigers were going to St. Louis. I was going to New Jersey.

The Detroit Tigers beat the shit out of the St. Louis Cardinals 13-1, and tied the series, at Busch Stadium. I listened to the game in the airport as I made my way to Fort Dix. The final game of the 1968 World Series was under way as Terry Wise and I boarded the airplane. The civilian charter airliner had reached altitude and I watched the Great Lakes pass under the fuselage through clear skies. We were headed for a refueling stop in Anchorage, Alaska.

Cloud cover thickened as we passed over Canada. When we finally approached Anchorage, the plane descended through the thick clouds revealing huge snow-covered mountains. We had reached our first stop. However, we were not allowed to go into the terminal while we waited for the plane's refueling procedure. Instead, for some unknown reason, we were ordered off the plane and expected to wait on the runway. Back at Fort Dix, in anticipation of our arrival in tropical Vietnam, we had been ordered to board the plane wearing our short-sleeved summer uniforms. The temperature, in Anchorage, hovered around freezing with light snow. So, the Alaskan version of *hurry-up and wait* mandated all the passengers running back and forth, in formation, on the tarmac. After a half hour of unanticipated exercise, shivering passengers found refuge in the now all-too-familiar confines of the freshly fueled airliner. No one could tell me who had won that last game of the World Series.

Our next stop—Yokota Air Base, Japan.

I had always wondered what Japan looked like. I still don't know. We had landed in thick fog at night. Just like Anchorage, there was no sheltered airport terminal. The weather in Japan was much warmer than Alaska. High humidity, associated with the fog, created dampness that was just short of rain. The foggy night air was claustrophobic as well as disorienting. This time, *hurrying-up to wait* involved sitting on bleachers under a corrugated metal roof. We were in a shelter with a cement floor and no walls. A fence, topped with barbed wire, was located behind the bleachers. There were lots of airplane noises accompanied by the smell of jet exhaust. Still, I spent an hour or so in Yokota Air Base and never saw the place.

Eventually the 120 uniformed passengers flopped back into the same seats we had strapped ourselves into fourteen hours ago. The only thing that had changed was the crew. No one, in the new group knew who had won the World Series. The prettiest stewardess I had ever seen, Rosemary Bradley, said that she would try to answer my baseball question before we landed in Vietnam. She never found out who had won the last baseball game.

Almost twenty-four hours after leaving Fort Dix the shinny aluminum time prison, disguised to look like a civilian airliner, descended into Vietnamese airspace through heavy overcast. The plane made a long low approach over a flat landscape composed of empty rice paddies. Late afternoon sunlight, its color spectrum filtered by thick clouds, gave the deserted fields a monotone Dracula-movie look. Random smoky black fires, burning in the growing dusk, magnified the malevolent effect. The airliner made a perfect landing and taxied to an effortless stop. The whole twenty-four hour journey ended so smoothly that it seemed like the flight hadn't really ended.

Since the aircraft didn't *feel* as though it stopped, maybe it never started. Perhaps the flight had never left Fort Dix New Jersey. Could there be an alternative scenario? Maybe this was a *Twilight Zone* trip. The whole trip could have been some kind of surreal illusion, like those 1950s military LSD tests. Could everyone have been tricked? Maybe we had been confined inside a metallic pressure vessel and not physically transported anywhere. I had been too excited to sleep during the entire trip. Evidently I was sleep-deprived. Could I have dozed-off and imagined the whole thing. I was dreaming.

In reality, our collective incarceration ended with a single door hissing open. We had arrived at Ton Son Heut Air Force Base just north of Saigon, not far from Long Binh. The dry air inside the airliner escaped in a depressurizing rush. Blue cigarette smoke was exchanged for another kind of mist. The new "fresh" air was hot and soggy with organic monsoon rain. This replacement atmosphere contrasted sharply with the stale dry air-conditioned atmosphere it displaced. The invisible difference in the air was more obvious than its temperature and moisture content. A heady mixture of odors was encapsulated in the water vapor that infiltrated into the airliner's cabin. Lack of sleep and jet lag combined, gave these new scents an almost psychedelic effect, pushing olfactory glands were forced into overdrive.

The odiferous mélange intensified with each snail's pace step toward the exit. The slow departure shuffle teased my nose as I approached the door. The plane's aluminum hatch opened onto a yet-to-be-explored alien universe. The curious new smells intensified with each step toward the exit, piquing my imagination.

The angelic flight attendant, Rosemary Bradley, had become a memorable friend during the last eight-hours of our journey. She had written her Pennsylvania address on a scrap of paper and promised to write. Now she was waving a cheerful farewell. My attention was rudely diverted. I was preoccupied with identifying the combination of pungent ingredients in the atmosphere. The new aromas had become a mephitic distraction. The exotic smells were undoubtedly holding valuable secrets about this alien land. My curiosity about the stink diverted my attention from the sad reality that I would never see Rosemary, again.

Jet fuel–*raw and cooked into exhaust*–were logically expected elements of this new world's odor. Indeed, heat and burnt fuel would be obvious ingredients in Hell's atmosphere. Humidity enhanced the heat. I squinted my eyes. The dimming late afternoon sunlight seemed glaring compared to the airliner's artificial luminescence. Strange smells that were a combination of rotting vegetation and mildew, mingled with the heavy air that enveloped me. More than trace amounts of human sweat were a component of Vietnam's exotic odors. Ingredients, emanating from unseen not-so-distant kitchens, were also involved in the heady perfume assaulting my olfactory sensors. However, there was an unusual element in this bouquet that was totally beyond anything I was familiar with. I would later learn that this was the reek released when human feces were burned in diesel fuel. No wonder that I found this particular redolence so elusive to identify; it certainly was disgusting to breathe. Surprisingly, like so many stomach-churning things I would encounter in Vietnam, I got used to it.

Even more surprising was that somehow my nose knew, before any of my other senses, that Vietnam was a place like no other.

DOING THE UNNECESSARY

How long do you Americans want to fight?
One year? Two years? Three years?
Five years? Ten years?
Twenty years?
We will be glad to accommodate you.

PHAM VAN DONG,
NORTH VIETNAMESE PRIME MINISTER 1966

DOING THE UNNECESSARY

Deplaning passengers were escorted to another set of bleachers under another sheet metal roof, similar to the area we had hurried to wait at in Japan. The sun had set while we waited for the Air Force to empty the civilian plane's cargo hold. After the obligatory *hurry-up and wait*, volunteers were chosen, from low ranking enlisted personnel. Terry and I were part of that *low-rank* category. But, after all those casual company formations back at Fort Benning, Terry and I managed to find a place to stand where we wouldn't become obvious work detail candidates. We successfully managed to <u>not</u> be selected for loading all the duffle bags into the idling unusual school bus.

These school bus transports were painted olive-drab green, not air-conditioned and featured heavy wire where there would have been windows. Steamy night air, passed through the substantially screened openings as we sped through deserted urban streets. The hour was late enough to be *officially* past curfew. Curfew meant that no local residents would welcome us as we proceeded to the Long Binh Replacement Center. Since there was no traffic, the buses traveled at high speed. We didn't stop at intersections or even slow down. The streets were eerily deserted. The buildings were dark with doorways additionally secured with rolling shutters or scissor gates. Widely spaced, glaring street lamps made the harsh shadows even more threatening. Storefronts secured with heavy shutters sported signage that was painted in an unreadable alien language. A strange urban landscape whipped past as we made our clandestine run through the sweltering night.

The Replacement (Repo) Center at Long Binh was a large compound. A twelve-foot-high chain-link fence, topped with razor sharp concertina wire, surrounded this military complex.

Regularly spaced guard towers lent a prison-like quality to this urban encampment. Was the fence designed to keep people out or hold us in? This facility featured a collection of cinderblock windowless barracks, set in straight precise military lines. The Replacement Center looked out of place. It was nothing like the densely packed stucco buildings in the surrounding neighborhood. The Repo Center appeared to have been bulldozed out of a low rent urban area, paved with asphalt, fortified and fenced.

Our assigned barracks was a two-story windowless cinderblock building. The interior was dimly lit with austere bare bulbs. Plastic yellow grill light fixtures, like the trouble lights in a garage, hung from insulated cords strung-out over the center aisle. The widely spaced glaring lights barely illuminated the long filthy room. Exotic tropical insects probably lurked in stark deep shadows. The ceiling was low, for a room of this size, and made the dark cavernous space feel even more oppressive. The unsealed concrete floor hadn't been swept recently and emitted a damp concrete mildew smell. Regulation metal bunk beds lined the walls. Cigarette butts, candy wrappers and dead roaches accented this room's seedy decor. The absence of footlockers made the center aisle look wider than the usual Army barracks. Mattresses, as usual, were rolled at the head of each bunk. There was no bedding, no sheets, no pillows or blankets, just thin military mattresses. Twenty-four hours of jet lag produced the kind of exhaustion that stifled complaint. We were allowed to *hurry-up and wait* for almost as long as it took for our jet lag to be replaced by boredom. Reveille was not sounded around these barracks.

Jetlag is disorienting. The longer the flight the worse you feel. After nearly twenty-four consecutive hours, and crossing the International Date Line, I didn't even know what day it was. I was only certain that I was hot and the sun had set. I found a bunk, slept and awoke to sunlight and even more heat. I had slept, fully clothed (except for shoes), on a mattress without sheets. Groggy, but not rested, I dug through my duffle bag found some fatigues, my shaving kit and made my way to the latrine.

The Mess Hall was my next priority, during lunch (I had slept through breakfast) I found out about the regular formations and unit assignments. I also discovered that the DETROIT TIGERS WON THE WORLD SERIES! They had beaten the St. Louis Cardinals, in game seven, by a score of four to one. It was so anticlimactic. The World Series, and an entire portion of my life, was over. After so much anticipation, why did I no longer care?

Two sweltering days later, Terry Wise and I were sent on our separate ways. Terry went south of Saigon. He drew an assignment with the Ninth Infantry Division. Terry was going to be wading through rice paddies around the Mekong River Delta. I went north. The First Infantry Division Replacement Depot at Di An was my next destination. We probably wouldn't meet again. It was amazing that we had journeyed together this far. Whatever happened, Terry and I promised to meet-up again in Louisville at the Zanza Bar.

Di An was about a half hour's ride, in the back of a truck, from Long Binh. The in-country training center was cleaner than the Repo Center. Here, the barracks were not buildings; they were tents similar to those in the TV program *M*A*S*H*. The replacement group's size diminished each time a formation was called. Clerks, cooks and truck drivers were siphoned-off and sent directly to their new units.

Before becoming Grunts, replacements attended in-country training. I was among the fresh infantry replacements. We listened to veterans present in-country seminars. We learned some Vietnamese phrases like "Halt!" (*Dung lie*) and "I surrender" (*Chew hoy*). We learned what booby-traps to watch for and the proper procedure for taking and interrogating prisoners. "Please" and "Thank You" were not included in our vocabulary lessons. However, the "good cop/bad cop" method of interrogation was demonstrated. Actual live enemy mines and booby-traps were displayed and available for close inspection. Finally, I was assigned to an even smaller group of GIs leaving for Lai Khe.

Lai Khe was thirty-five miles north of Saigon, the tiny village was completely encapsulated within an expansive encampment. The Base Camp for the First Infantry Division (aka the Big Red One) was many times larger than the small village nestled in its center. The Big Red One Base Camp and Headquarters had once been a 'company town' for the Michelin Rubber Company.

The southeast corner of the huge First Infantry Division base camp was where Charlie Company, 1st BN of the 16th Infantry called home. However, the Company was never "home." Bandido Charlie was continually *out in the field*. October marked the end of the rainy season. The Charlie Company area in Lai Khe was a sea of foot-deep muddy goo. Bandido Charlie was a mechanized company; meaning it traveled on tracks as in Armored Personnel Carriers. When it rained, during the months-long monsoon season, Charlie Company's tracked vehicles churned dusty roads into thick muddy ooze. Even in the Company's absence there was enough traffic to maintain the deep mud field. Eventually, the rainy season would end and the clay/mud would dry into a concrete hard surface. Then the heavy tracked vehicles Charlie Company used would grind the hardened surface into a fine choking dust.

Replacements were fed and assigned a locker. The locker warehoused our duffle bags and meager personal belongings. After exactly one night in the company area I was loaded into a duce and a half, with a half-dozen other replacements and trucked north on Vietnam's main (only) paved highway. We caught up with Bandido Charlie at a firebase next to the roadside. I was assigned to a squad and mostly left alone. The shuffling and dealing was finally done. This was the hand I had been dealt–*the end of the line*.

My real in-country education lay ahead. There was so much to learn.

First, replacements weren't particularly liked.

Replacement resentment was logical. Fucking New Guys (FNGs) were inexperienced and therefore more likely to make mistakes. In a combat environment, mistakes could be lethal. Errors were not only deadly to the newbie but their foul-ups could kill unlucky squad-mates as well. Moreover, why be friendly to someone who was very likely to get you killed or hospitalized?

Additionally, FNGs were too clean. A spotless set of clothes and polished boots were like a neon sign that read, "*I just got here. Please shoot me.*" A clean uniform advertised a replacement's in-country bewilderment, as well as their ignorance. New guys smelled of soap and aftershave in a place where everyone else smelled *really bad*. A clean smell could give away one's location, especially at night, no matter how good their concealment skills. Therefore, cleanliness was not 'next to Godliness' (although it could get you closer to God a little ahead of schedule).

Moreover, a replacement was taking the place of someone the squad had known, trusted and was familiar. The guy the FNG replaced was more than a member of their team. He had been part of their family. They had liked him a lot. They had been through a lot together. Everyone in the squad had felt pain when a teammate had died or was wounded. He might have saved someone's life or just made it through his tour and was heading home. Whatever the reason, the veteran would be missed. A replacement almost *always* had big shoes to fill.

FNGs hadn't been trained to be mechanized Grunts, Infantry training makes straight-leg Grunts. Being mechanized involved some not-so-subtle differences.

Reaction to a sniper would have been an example of that distinction. Straight legs are trained to take cover, determine the sniper's location, return fire, hunt the bastard down and eliminate him. A mechanized unit response is slightly different, ending with the same results–for the sniper.

A short time after my assignment to Charlie Company some Viet Cong snipers, holed up in a tree line, shot at our column. All the tracks simply stopped. Bandido Charlie went into action like a well-oiled machine. Forty-eight Armored Personnel Carriers turned, as one, toward the snipers. All the 50-caliber machine guns started firing at the same time.

I grabbed a M-16 and hopped off the track along with everyone else. In all the noise and smoke, I didn't see that I was the only one going after the sniper, as I had been trained. Our track's 50-caliber. Gunner, eventually got my attention by shooting just over my head. He kept putting rounds close in around me in an attempt to get me to come back (there was no point in trying to shout to me in all the racket). Finally, I came back to the group, huddled behind the Armored Personnel Carrier (APC) and waited with everyone else in my squad.

After the shooting stopped, the same machine gunner who had recently beckoned to me with ½" copper jacked rounds, called me over. He showed me an AK-47-round wedged between the machine gun's shroud and its frame. Before he told me how the bullet got there he asked me what I thought I had been doing. I explained. Apparently, while he was trying to signal me to come back, one of the snipers had been shooting at him. That bullet, jammed between his gun and its surrounding shield, had been that sniper's parting gift. The gunner advised me to never run out in front of the track again. It was sage advice. I only had to be told once.

The next time (we were sniped at regularly), I vowed to learn by paying closer attention to the rest of the squad. A firefight is an incredibly isolating event. A combination of gun smoke, bullets and loud weapons create a kind of chaos that is not conducive to educational enlightenment. Furthermore, there would have been no one to ask. The squad had more pressing concerns. Incoming munitions always rated a higher priority than taking a neophyte aside for some kind of teachable moment. Everyone except the driver and the 50-caliber gunner hopped off the track. They gathered behind the shield provided by the protective mass of the Armored Personnel Carrier. Most of the squad just hung-out, calmly taking a smoke break while waiting for the shooting to stop. A few guys popped-out from cover, took pot shots at the snipers with M-16s and ducked back in behind the track. If it had been a serious attack, everyone would have spread-out away from the track and laid down some real fire. This was just a couple of snipers, routine assholes with a death-wish. The 50-caliber machine guns always eliminated snipers. When multiple 50-caliber machine guns concentrate fire into a tree line, the trees disintegrate, smoke and, thanks to burning phosphorous tracers, catch fire. The 50-caliber machine gunners didn't really need any help from the rest of the squad; the enemy snipers never had a chance.

It is often said that you don't hear the bullet that kills you. That may be so, but I can testify that you can definitely hear the bullet that barely misses you. I can't describe the sound exactly—the loudest thunder clap/explosion you've ever heard—right next to your ear. It certainly got my undivided attention. The noise was loud enough to make me reflexively ducked down out of sight behind the cover of some very dense waist-high grass. It took a fraction of a second to realize that a bullet had come very close to taking my head clean off. "Frightened" would be understating my initial sensation by a magnitude of about a million. This was one of those "fight or flight" moments. What to do next? Run? That would only have meant being shot in the back. More bullets came zipping over my head.

I was sprawled out, trying to will myself into a foxhole that didn't exist. I needed to focus. Some son of a bitch was really trying to kill me! What exactly was I going to do about it? I didn't have much time for reflection. I GOT ANGRY! More than just 'mad,' I became enraged. Becoming angrier than I have ever been created a huge adrenalin rush. I was going to kill that son of a bitch. If I had to rip his damn head off with my bare hands, that bastard was going to die. Then suddenly I realized that I happened to be holding a loaded M-16–*just what I needed*.

After I decided that I was going to have to kill this asshole, it seemed logical to move a couple of feet from the place where he had drawn a bead on me. I crawled a couple feet, poked my head up for an instant and got a bearing on the flash from the muzzle of his gun. The shooter must have thought that he had shot me because his attention had shifted to another target. His green tracer bullets were no longer landing in my immediate vicinity. I stayed in a crouch and raised my head up again. My eyes were just a little higher than the grass that concealed me. This time I had my weapon ready, round in the chamber and the safety off. It seemed to take forever to find his muzzle flash again and line him up in my sights. He was at the base of the tree line. I had intentionally set the selector switch on my M-16 to *semi*, as opposed to *auto*, not wanting to shoot my wad in one long burst. I fired five shots in rapid succession. The fifth round was a tracer. I watched my tracer ricochet off some unseen blade of grass half way to my intended target. I had missed the son of a bitch by miles. I tried again. Luckily, there were no friendly aircraft in the area. Each time I drew a bead and fired, my shots made a sharp right angle turn straight up into the sky. I was hitting something that deflected my bullets. Every round ricocheted straight up long before it came anywhere near the target. It was like this gook was behind some kind of invisible shield! This jerk just put a round within inches of my head and I was unable to put anything anywhere near him. Now I was double pissed.

Anger compounded my frustration. My exasperation centered on the sudden realization that an M-16 was as useless as a rabbit-gun. The *something* that was deflecting my bullets was just flimsy grass.

The M-16 fires a 22-caliber magnum round. The bullet is tiny and lightweight compared to the enemy's heavier 30-caliber ammunition. It's the "magnum" designation that is supposed to compensate for the M-16's weenie bullet size. As a "magnum" the brass casing holding the propellant gunpowder is much longer than a regular 22-caliber rifle cartridge kids shoot after they trade-in their BB gun. The M-16's larger "magnum" casing holds an extra portion of gunpowder. The extra powder forces the flyweight bullet to leave the gun barrel at extreme velocity. The exceptionally fast moving projectile is supposed to compensate for the bullet's lack of mass. When an M-16 round hits a person, it tumbles and causes massive amounts of damage and injury. In theory, this sounds great. There is only one problem: the lightweight bullet is very easily deflected. A single blade of grass, between the shooter and the target, is enough to change a hit into a miss. Vietnam has a lot of grass. Still, despite all this, an M-16 is slightly better than nothing.

Shortly after learning this lesson about the inadequacies of the M-16, I volunteered to carry my squad's M-60 machine gun. Nobody else wanted to use the M-60 anyway. It was heavy to carry, weighing more than twice as much as an M-16. The M-60's ammunition was heavy too, came in belts and had sharp connecting links. But one belt had the same number of bullets as five twenty-round M-16 magazines. I was probably a higher priority target for the enemy too (because there was a higher probability that I would take them out). The M-60 fired a heavier 30-caliber bullet that was equal to the enemy's AK-47. My M-60 rounds were not easily deflected away from their target. A bullet being diverted by a blade of grass was never a problem with the M-60. I pretty much always hit what I aimed at.

Armored Personnel Carrier from Bandido Charlie 1st BN 16th Inf in the Michelin Rubber Plantation, 1969.

MECHANIZED RULES

N obody in Vietnam rode inside an Armored Personnel Carrier or APC.

There was one exception: the track driver, he had no choice. The driver had to sit on a small seat, usually having the top half of his head exposed. Everyone in the squad had to learn to drive the track in case something happened to the driver. The controls were rudimentary. There was no brake pedal or steering wheel. Two vertical sticks, laterals, controlled the tracks. The laterals default position was straight up for neutral. Push both laterals forward, while pressing down on the accelerator, and the vehicle would move forward. Push the right lateral forward, leaving the left one alone, and the vehicle would turn left. Push the left lateral forward, leaving the right one alone, and the vehicle would turn right. Pulling back on both laterals was reverse (no mirrors or back-up cameras, or brakes). You could coast to a stop or pull back on both laterals to stop in a hurry. The track would pivot in place by pushing one lateral forward and pulling the other one back. The regular driver did the track's maintenance and made sure the track's tank was filled with diesel fuel.

The rest of the squad rode on the flat deck of the APC, behind the driver and the 50-caliber machine gun. The gunner sat over an open hatch. He used the edge of the hatch opening as a seat. The hatch cover, upholstered with sandbags and flack jackets, formed a seat back. The whole set-up rotated like an open turret with a heavy metal shroud shielding the gunner. Both the gunner and driver wore helmets fitted with headsets to communicate with each other and all the other tracks. The rear three-quarter of the APC's horizontal top surface was upholstered with sandbags and flack jackets. The green bags of sand did not provide cushioning. The track's movement, bouncing and vibration, compacted the sand and formed

GIs from Bandido Charlie hanging out in a firebase.

hard rounded semi-reclined *seats*. Flack jackets provided minimal cushioning; flack jackets were originally designed to be worn like a vest. They were not bullet-proof, might stop some shrapnel and did make a very warm fashion statement. The ensconced riders were minimally protected from unforgiving metal angular edges by the sandbags. A near reclining posture distributed the bouncing jolts of the moving metal box they were riding on. This horizontal arrangement provided the riders a lower, less visible, profile while keeping riders from bouncing off the pitching deck. The spaces between the sandbags was littered with flack jackets, M-16s, ammunition boxes for the 50-caliber, 20-round magazines for the M-16s, canteens, and C-Rations. All of the equipment was readily accessible and communal. Anyone could grab the nearest M-16 and anticipate that it would be loaded and ready to go. The biggest advantage to riding on top of the track was rapid egress. Egress from the deck of the APC was not always elective.

Sometime mines and booby-traps would simply eject the riders. The rapidity of ejection was incumbent on the size of the mine. Bandido Charlie, on average, lost one track a week to 'large' mines. Most of the time we found 'small' anti-personnel mines, the kind

that were designed to simply maim a passer-by. The Viet Cong figured that wounding a GI consumed more of our resources than killing a GI. A wounded man would mean having to stop and tend his wounds with the additional "benefit" (to the enemy) of giving away our location. A helicopter would be needed to fly in for the medical evacuation. So the enemy planted lots of 'small' mines as well as some really BIG ones. An armored personnel carrier was a considerable shield against those smaller anti-personnel mines and was way better than setting one off at ground level. That's not to say that being blown or "ejected" from the top of an APC is a pleasant experience. At least, riding on top of an armored personnel carrier offered some chance of survival. Riding inside an APC increased the odds of becoming a casualty, considerably. Even a 'minor' explosive event, could transform a track's normally white interior surfaces into a Jackson Pollack paint study in red.

BANDIDO CHARLIE

When Bandido Charlie was stationed north of Lai Khe, we patrolled on or about Highway One. This road was Vietnam's major north-south highway. It ran nearly the length of the entire country. We were assigned a section of two-lane blacktop. Every day, at first light, we made sure that Charlie (the bad Charlie) hadn't mined our section of road during the night. The methods we used were: a) sweeping the highway with a metal detector or b) "thundering" the road with some tracks. Both methods could be hazardous. However, "thundering" the road was faster and a whole lot more fun. Two or three tracks would line up side-by-side spanning the width of the road. Then they would speed off down the road like some kind of *Road Warrior* drag race. The mines, if there were any, would turn up one-way or another. The remainder of the day would be spent spread out along the roadside guarding pavement. At night we would put out ambush patrols.

Shortly after my first week with Charlie Company, I was assigned a position in an old-fashion slow-walking mine sweeping team. I was one of a dozen or so people walking along the sides of the road protecting the minesweeper. The sweeper methodically went about his work checking the road's surface with a metal detector. The sweeper concentrated on changes in pitch. He listened, through his metal detector's earphones, to a pitch that would change when the detector's electromagnet passed over the metal in a mine's detonator.

Subtle shifts in sound would indicate a buried mine. He remained very focused on his job. The rest of the team made sure that he wasn't distracted by anyone shooting at him.

An earth-shaking explosion interrupted our morning walk. I dropped into a crouch. The chest high weeds, where I happened to be standing, offered total concealment. The explosion could have marked the start of an ambush. Green tracers could be coming my way any moment. Instead, for the longest time, there was only

Image by Tony Hallas

silence. I poked my head up. Screams of agony came from the grass where the fifth man, on my side of the road, had been standing. I had been the third man, on one side of the road, walking in the V-shaped formation with the minesweeper on point. The fourth person, walking behind me, had vanished. His position was now marked by a dissipating wisp of smoke. The man who had been immediately behind me had set off a mine and was *gone*. I had walked right past the mine that got him. The fifth man in line, walking behind the very recently departed number four man, was wounded and in considerable pain. A medic came to him from the road.

I was sort of stunned when the mine went off. I didn't know what had happened. Initially, I thought that I was about to be shot. After a period of prolonged silence it became obvious that wasn't going to happen. I started to make my way back to the wounded guy through the grass. GIs gathering on the road shouted for me to stop. They knew that I was standing in an old overgrown minefield. The tall grass was probably concealing more trip wires.

Medics has already come to the aid of the wounded and carried him to a cleared portion of the road. A dust-off chopper came and went. During all the commotion, I was pretty much ignored and just stood there awaiting further instructions.

Eventually the road surface was cleared of mines. The same could not be said for the shoulder of the road where I was still standing. The weeds were too high and thick to use the mine sweeper and clear a path to my *perilous* position. My squad gathered on the road. They didn't exactly offer any solutions for my predicament. Instead, they ignored my inquiries for a solution to my mine situation and made bets about the odds of the FNG (me) making it out of the grass and down to the safety of the paved road. Cliff Poris had obviously bet on me not making it to the road.

I shouted to Cliff, "Hey! I'm standin' in a minefield here!"

Cliff Poris, originally from Brooklyn, was a long time veteran member of my squad. Cliff had been with Bandido Charlie when Charlie Company was part of the Ninth Division roaming the Mekong Delta, south of Saigon. Cliff shouted his suggestion to me. He thought that I should just walk down to the road. I didn't believe that he was serious, because he was laughing, with the other guys, just before he offered his resolution to my problem.

I reminded him, with an indignant New Yorker *Ratso Rizzo* impersonation, "I'm standin' in a minefield! Perhaps someone could inquire about having me lifted out here with a helicopter, or something?"

Cliff laughed some more. He thought that the only way I would get a chopper to come, and haul my ass out, would be by setting off another mine. My sniggering mentor modified his earlier suggestion, shouting that it might help to run as opposed to walk down to the road. That way an exploding mine would be behind me and might actually blow whatever remaining parts of my body forward onto the road. The guys, standing safely on the road, saw the dark humor in his suggestion. They laughed. I didn't appreciate their jocularity. There was the distinct probability that I might be killed or maimed

Image by Tony Hallas

if I accepted Cliff's absurd advice. Then again, I didn't have much choice.

My audience grew impatient. I took Cliff's suggestion and ran down to the road.

When I was standing safely on the road, Cliff put his arm on my shoulder and asked, "Are you sure that you're not from New York?"

"Naw," I said with a smile, "I know who my father is!"

I was no longer a FNG. We both laughed and have been best friends ever since.

Life in the Mechanized Infantry became routine. Mornings started with sweeping the road. Days were devoted to guarding, blocking and/or patrolling around the road (using reconnaissance patrols of various sizes). Nights were a rotating sequence of ambush patrol, listening post or guard inside the wire that formed the fire support base. At night, sleep was divided into small segments that never exceeded one-hour in every three.

FIREBASE JIM

Every firebase had a name. Charlie Company had spent a couple of weeks at Firebase Julie before we moved-on to Firebase Jim. Fire support bases were temporary strongholds. Razor wire formed a circular outer barrier. The wire was rigged with flares, booby-traps and mines. Firebases usually had a single gated entrance. Inside the Firebase, a formidable series of obstacles made the layered defense system almost impenetrable. A band of sandbagged foxholes were positioned between the wire and another interior ring of armored personnel carriers. The APCs were parked behind their own individual chain-link fence barriers. These chain-link fences acted as shields and were intended to detonate enemy rocket propelled grenades (RPGs) before the rocket reached the APC. The inner-most circle of the encampment was where the command post, cooks, mortar platoon and two M-60 tanks were located. Every night four three-man teams went "outside the wire" on listening post. Firebase Jim was located in a defensible clearing with clear lanes of fire on all sides. Firebase Jim was very close to the Highway One.

Firebase Jim was a functioning base camp before Bandido Charlie moved into its rustic confines. It had all the regular elements that were included in all firebases: concertina wire boundary, gun emplacements and latrines–most of the essentials were already there. We just dug more holes and added more sandbags to make the place feel more *homey*. Firebase Jim did sport one unusual, and unique, additional feature. Firebase Jim presented Bandido Charlie with one established close neighbor: a very dead Vietnamese man.

He was lying on the shoulder of the road thirty or forty yards away from the gate. Jim is not a Vietnamese name. The firebase definitely wasn't named after him. But, since he was there before we got there and he obviously couldn't object, we named him Jim. Jim was wearing black pants and a white shirt when he died. We couldn't tell how old he was or what killed him. He might have been a Viet Cong who died in a firefight or just road kill. Either way, Jim was just laying there, on the side of the road, when we moved in. The heavy traffic on the road whizzed passed. Dead Vietnamese were not our responsibility. We left him for the Vietnamese to take care of. Unfortunately, the Vietnamese were just as good as we were at ignoring Jim.

However, as time passed, Jim became harder to ignore. The scent of his natural decomposition gradually grew into an invisible dome that permeated the atmosphere surrounding the Firebase. Jim "the Gook" was with us all the time; not in the spiritual sense. His redolence was with us when we ate and slept. He managed to overpower the stench from our latrines. Jim had done something the enemy was unable to do. All by himself Jim had surrounded the entire Firebase.

Listening Posts (LP) were our after dark early warning system. Every night four lightly armed three-man teams, with radios, were assigned to sit outside of the Firebase perimeter and used the radio to sound an early warning of an impending attack. Beside a radio, the teams only carried M-16s and claymore mines for protection. LPs silently watched for enemy movement. Their armament was light because they were not supposed to fight. The teams' function was to report enemy presence and return to the relative safety *inside* the wire. If they didn't make it back in time, the listeners would run a very real risk of being caught in crossfire and become victims of friendly fire.

As if potentially being shot by our own side wasn't bad enough, Jim, the dead dink, was an invisible presence. Like a haunting spirit, his stench would materialize, out of nowhere, when it was least expected. One hundred degree plus daytime temperatures expedited Jim's putrefaction. He seemed to get riper with each passing hour. Jim's corpse began to swelled-up after his second day in the sun. Apparently, continuous traffic on the highway detoured daytime scavengers. We shot anything that came near the firebase at night. Eventually, Jim's bloated body became a logistical conundrum. No one could stand being close to him long enough to dig a grave that he could be pushed into. If we dug a hole somewhere else, there was no way to move his bloated jelly-like putrefying remains to the hole.

Jim was with us for the entire two weeks we occupied Firebase Jim. Physically Jim had bloated out and doubled his original size. Reek-wise, the corpse was thousands of times larger; Jim was totally off any metric describing disgusting stench. He was particularly poignant at night.

Cool evening breezes usually brought welcome relief from the sweltering daytime temperatures. At Firebase Jim, I preferred dead calm. Somehow, after dark, even the lightest breeze positioned my nose downwind from Jim. Two nights out of three Cliff and I were outside of Firebase Jim's perimeter wire and never far away enough to be out of its stink range.

My distain for our platoon Sergeant had ensnared Cliff and myself in a web of unescapable retaliation. The incompetent moron in charge of our platoon established our predictable routine: one night inside the Firebase, Ambush Patrol the next night followed by Listening Post duty every third night. Cliff and I became a two-man listening post team to prevent some other unsuspecting GI from becoming ensnared in the Sergeant's web of recrimination. After having worked listening post several times, we declared that we didn't need to bring a third guy with us. Just the two of us would be designated as a Listening Post team. Cliff and I watched each other's back, in one-hour shifts. Our set-up was an unusual variation from the more conventional three-man arrangement.

Cliff and I rarely reported enemy movement. However, Cliff did manage to shake me out of a sound sleep on the one occasion when he had seen someone running in a counter clockwise direction around the Firebase. The movement was about twenty yards away. *That was really close!* At that range, the guy would have almost tripped over the detonator wires that were connected to our claymore mines. We were concealed under a bush. Cliff wanted me to call in his sighting. I refused. In an urgent whisper, I explained that since he had seen the guy, he should call it in. We didn't argue. Cliff was excited and did not speak clearly into the radio's microphone. The person trying to decipher his report in the Command Post, couldn't understand what Cliff was telling him. I was a little surprised when Captain Goldberg came on the horn and asked to talk to me. He wanted me to relay Cliff's report. As I was speaking, the perimeter guards on the opposite side of the camp opened fire. We instantly received permission to leave our post and come back into the camp. We didn't have to be told a second time. The camouflaged gate was even harder to find in the darkness. Jim, the dead Dink, provided an aromatic guide point. Cliff and I followed our noses and were careful to not get too close to our invisible guide. The commotion on the other side of the perimeter had made all of the men in the base's interior firing positions more than a little *jumpy*.

Once inside the Firebase, we prepared for an attack that never happened. The VC Cliff had seen, was just a probe. He was checking to see if we were awake. Knowing that the enemy was out there, checking us out, made Cliff and me a little reluctant to go back out for the rest of our shift. We were assured, despite having sounded the initial alarm, that we'd still have to go back. Besides, there was a problem: we had left our listening post in a bit of a hurry and hadn't blown our claymore mines.

Apparently, we were supposed to have set off our mines *before* we came back into the base. Nobody told us. Now the company Sergeant was telling us. Because we had left the mines out there we were going to have to go back out and find them. Yes, in the dark and with verified enemy movement; Cliff and I were going to make sure that the VC hadn't simply taken the explosive mines we had errantly not detonated. Or, worse yet, they might have simply turned our claymores around so they would kill us if and when we detonated them. There was also the possibility that our mines had been discovered and booby-trapped so they would go off when we picked them up. The Company Sergeant patiently reminded us of the reasons why we had to go back and wished us luck. We stealthily slipped past the gate out into a sleepless, and otherwise uneventful, night.

After two stinking weeks at Firebase Jim, Bandido Charlie was sent to its next assignment. We did not leave Firebase Jim the way we found it. Someone had found a solution for Jim the Vietnamese guy. As Bandido Charlie Company departed at a reverent pace past Jim's body, a single armored personnel carrier, with a single gas mask clad rider and identically protected driver, pulled-up and stopped next to Jim's revolting remains. Diesel fuel was poured over Jim. A flare was lit and dropped. The petroleum fueled pyre was ignited. Jim was cremated. Jim's raising plume of black funerary smoke mingled with our exhaust. The combined vapors formed a putrid incense that dissipated as we accelerated away from Firebase Jim, leaving only dust and exhaust in our wake.

JHAT

Unlike Charlie Company's command Sergeant; our Platoon Sergeant was an asshole. In fact, the two non-commissioned officers were polar opposites. The top Sergeant was a hard, but fair, seasoned veteran. The Platoon Sergeant was an inexperienced graduate from some NCO school, who used his position to avoid doing any actual work. The Platoon Sergeant and I shared a mutual dislike from the moment we met. Obviously his alma mater hadn't been the Fort Benning NCO School. This blonde California surfer frat-boy Sergeant had never seen that shoulder patch that said, 'FOLLOW ME.' He was a 'lead from the rear' boss who simply covered his own ass. Cliff and I paid a handsome price for my disdain. My scorn resulted in extra lousy duty in a place where extra work led to more sleep deprivation. We did more listening posts and ambush patrols than anyone else in our squad. It was my fault. Cliff never complained.

Somehow blondie-surfer Platoon Sergeant was too cheerful when he announced that our squad was going back to Lai Khe a little earlier than everyone else. Something had to be up. Our sergeant had *volunteered* us—the whole squad this time—for another "special" detail.

Bandido Charlie was going back to Lai Khe for re-supply. The *good news* was that the sergeant had volunteered our track to go back a little sooner than everyone else. We were going to be one of the first tracks to leave. Therefore our track might be first getting back. We could be first in line for showers, clean clothes and hot food. The *bad news*–we would be one of two APCs escorting a third 'questionable' APC *Meaning* the 'questionable' track might/probably break down. If it did break down, we would have to hang around guarding it until a tank retrieval unit came out from Lai Khe to pick it up. The smiling Platoon Sergeant wished us Good Luck.

Of course, the track the Platoon Sergeant was riding on was not going to be part of the guard detail that he had blithely volunteered my squad for. Additionally, Sarge hadn't mentioned, if we wound up guarding the broken down track, our reward would be arriving late into Lai Khe, *after* the rest of the Company. This would mean that our payoff for an extra long day (spent posing as sitting ducks on the roadside), would be a mess hall serving cold cuts and leftovers, a trickle of water for a shower and bunks that were unclaimed because they were next to the overflowing shit-burning latrines.

It was still dark at 0400 hours when our squad's escort-duty day started. The cooks hadn't been re-supplied. We got no breakfast—*not even coffee*. Our track didn't have its usual reserve boxes of C-rations. After all, we were on our way to be re-supplied. We rolled out of the firebase gate, our empty stomachs were fueled by optimism. The road had not been swept for mines.

Our morale was still buoyed by the off chance of getting back to the Company area early. We optimistically pictured ourselves at the Enlisted Men's Club showered, wearing clean fatigues and drinking ice-cold beers before everyone else arrived.

Two miles down the dusty road, our cheerful dreams evaporated like the dew on the morning grass. The *questionable* Armored Personnel Carrier we were escorting resolved the issue of who would arrive in Lai Khe first. There was no long any question; *questionable* had sputtered to a stop. We sat motionless listening to waking birds and the grumblings of our empty stomachs. Now we were just one of three APCs parked by the side of the road, just one of three squads silently watching another spectacular sunrise in paradise.

Two hours into our daytime guard duty, Bandido Charlie sped past. Smiling men– *riding on speeding tracks*–cheered, waved and called out a greeting that sounded like *Suckers*. They whipped by leaving us in a cloud of dust and diesel fumes. For a while, the ground-shaking rumble of their passing almost drowned out the sounds of our empty stomachs.

It was another glorious sunny day, 0700 hours and the temperature was already in the low nineties, well on its way to the usual hundred plus. This was not a dry heat. Fortunately, the shadows cast by some nearby trees afforded some early protection from the morning sun. That reprieve would pass as the morning wore on.

While on patrol in the rice paddies between Di An and Saigon, PFC Vincent Camarda temps these children. They are not begging for candy–their focus is an American cigarette.

Civilian traffic grew heavier as the sun climbed into the cloudless blue sky. We knew that food would probably be coming our way and probably wouldn't come with the 'tank retrieval unit.' Breakfast was most likely to arrive riding on that wave of humanity that would eventually sweep past our cluster of vehicles. Vietnamese were big on setting-up roadside concession stands catering to the passing traveler's every need. When Charlie Company guarded the road, street vendors seemed to be everywhere. Surely it would only be a matter of time before someone selling something to eat would notice us as they passed. All kinds of stuff were available for a price–*anytime*. Our guts were empty, so there was plenty of room for hope.

However, our wait for the right kind of vendor wasn't happening as quickly as we had desired. At first, people wanted to sell us cigarettes, the one item we had. The next wave of traveling concessionaires was stocked with food made for local tastes. They sold weird Vietnamese food, like fertile eggs, that had been buried in hot sand to 'cook.' No one on our track was hungry enough to consider eating the blackened chicks preserved inside eggshells. Just the smell that emanated from one of those fertilized sand-baked eggs inspired fasting. Vendors selling beer had also found their way to our position. But it was too early for beer, especially on an empty stomach.

Finally, some curious kids came out from a nearby collection of huts. One bashful seven-year-old barefoot boy, wearing black shorts, approached the parked APCs. His white shirt was sewn from the silky fabric that had once been a parachute from an artillery flare. The youngster overcame his shyness long enough to ask for a cigarette. Somebody gave him one. He didn't speak English very well. Through sign language, and pidgin Vietnamese, we were able to communicate that there was money to be made by finding something we could eat and/or drink. He ran home delighted with his potential of contributing to his family's welfare.

The kid eventually returned with some Cokes, ice and a submarine-shaped sandwich. The Vietnamese apparently had learned the art of bread making from our French predecessors. His torpedo sandwich was made from a baguette almost three feet long. The bread was so fresh that it was still warm. The crunchy-crusted sandwich was filled with lettuce and gray mystery meat covered with spicy hot sauce. We had been taught to haggle, as a matter of saving face, but the little guy was so cute and we were ravenous. This nice little kid had earned his full asking price. I paid, snatched-up the sandwich and ripped it in half. My portion was gone before Cliff climbed down from his vantage point on top of the track. I was already savoring one of the two ice cold Cokes I had purchased. Cliff queried me, through a mouth full of sandwich, about the sub's ingredients. He repeated his question still chewing on his meal. Opening the sandwich and pushing aside the lettuce, he pointed to the gray meat suspended in some kind of gelatinous substance and asked, "What kind of meat is this?"

"I don't know." I replied, "It tasted like head cheese to me."

Cliff didn't believe that the Vietnamese made lunch meat, much less head cheese.

So, I asked the delivery boy, "What kind of meat is in this sandwich?"

It took a while for him to understand the question. Opening the last fragments of Cliff's sandwich, I patiently repeated the question pointing to a small particle of the oddly shaped substance.

Recognition flashed across the boy's cherubic countenance as he gave his one word answer, "jhat."

Now it was my turn to not understand.

He just repeated, "jhat."

We went around again, "No bic (*understand*) JHAT" I said. He kept saying, "jhat."

Finally, it occurred to me that maybe he could show me a 'jhat.' I picked up a twig, smoothed away some gravel and asked the kid to draw a picture of a 'jhat' in the roadside dirt.

This little urchin had some genuine artistic potential. However, the simple sketch he had drawn in the dirt displayed more than his ability to make pictures; it also illustrated that he really had a problem pronouncing the English letter 'R'. Cliff had been correct. Vietnamese do not make headcheese. We stared, in disbelief, at the animal the little boy had beautifully scratched into the dust. It was a **RAT**!

I had eaten half of a rat sandwich. Cliff didn't finish the small portion that remained of his half-sandwich. In fact, he returned the portion he had already eaten. The bread was probably still warm.

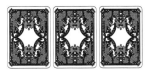

ANOTHER SHUFFLE

Rest and Resupply in the Company area, at Lai Khe, lasted two days. That was two days for those who hadn't *helped* with guarding the broken down track. Those who had baby-sat the lame APC returned to base considerably later than everyone else. The predicted price paid for our dalliance had indeed reduced our time at the Enlisted Men's Club. Everything else had gone pretty much as expected. The Mess Hall only offered cold cuts (at least they weren't gray), we were last into the showers and got the less-than-choice bunks.

Someone had broken the lock off of my locker and had stolen the last of my personal possessions. Everything was gone, including my photographs. They even took the images of my family as well as that picture from my locker back at Fort Polk. I didn't really care. The stuff had sentimental value. But, after all, it was just stuff.

We left Lai Khe to go south on a Company-sized Reconnaissance-in-force, Bandido Charlie was going to be redeployed in the Michelin Rubber Plantation. We were headed into a vast area of rubber trees and jungle. This was going to be a big change in routine. Our new mission would be even more dangerous than guarding the road.

Before the re-supply, and the broken-down track, Cliff had volunteered us to go on a smaller, platoon-sized reconnaissance. Since we were volunteers, Cliff and I did not ride on our regular squad's track. We had become part of an exploratory expedition to checkout the Michelin Rubber Plantation. That particular ride in the woods ended badly.

Four APCs and a Tiger tank formed a re-enforced mechanized platoon. The sun was blazing out of a cloudless blue sky as our armed band made its way on either side of a trail. We followed a two-track (it was in a remote area and too under-used to be considered a "road") as it meandered through a wide clearing in the rubber trees. The tank was centered in the formation with two APCs flanking it, front and rear, on either side.

The armored personnel carrier, in the front right corner of our little reconnaissance formation, hit a mine. The explosion was deafening. We felt the force from a powerful concussion wave as it passed over the trailing track we rode on. This mine was not some small anti-personnel mine—It was a **BIG** explosive devise.

In addition to C-rations and non-lethal supplies, all APCs carried ammunition, grenades, fuel, C4 plastic explosives and stuff that could easily turn a tracked vehicle into a bomb. APCs have heavy aluminum slabs for armor. Aluminum armor plates can stop most bullets, however it is nowhere near as protective as a tank's armor. None of that mattered because this particular mine could have easily taken out a tank. The explosion was huge. Everything instantly stopped. Time seemed to slow-down. Events occurred, from that explosive instant slow motion forward, in a thick gooey blur. Every horrific detail was revealed with excruciating stop-action frame by frame precision.

Cliff and I jumped off the track we were riding on. Our preparation, for any impending attack, was temporarily interrupted by a mesmerizing black donut-shaped cloud that was slowly raising over the wreckage that had once been an APC. Flames and debris rolled over inside a strange black smoke-ring. The hoop from hell slowly ascended into the sky. This thing rolled onto itself and seemed to develop more mass as it temporarily loomed over the burning wreckage. Then, its diameter grew and density diminished as it slowly began its ascent. The circle of smoke leisurely drifted upward over the wreckage. Initially, a thinning column of black smoke connected the expanding fiery ring to the burning hulk below. The black smoke and orange flames contrasted sharply with the bright azure blue sky. It appeared that the roiling ring from hell was slowed, in its ascent over the trees, by the heavy solid objects trapped in the smoke and flames. Flecks of green nylon flack jackets, tumbled in the flaming debris.

The slow motion illusion ended with the realization that men were inside those olive drab flack jackets. People were engulfed in that smoking angry red-orange band of death and destruction. Men had been caught-up, along with fragments of broken weapons, dirt and burning fuel. People and material were reduced to burning debris and blasted up over the trees. Everything that had been on, or inside, that armored personnel carrier was now climbing upward in a reluctantly raising halo from hell, churning toward the heavens over the treetops. Some of the men, on their way into the heavens, hadn't died, yet. Cliff and I heard them screaming. Trapped in a smoking circle, catapulted into the sky. Boys, who would never become men, cried-out in agony. Their screams didn't sound human.

Helplessly, we listened to their tormented shrieks. Hearing those screams was unavoidable. I could not force myself not to watch. Burning dismembered men ascended to a tortured apex before streaking back down to earth and certain death. To those devastated dying men, death had to have been a merciful end to their burning agony. I looked over at Cliff. I will never forget the look on his face. The screaming must have stopped when the bodies slammed into the trees. For me, the screams will never completely stop. I *will always hear their tormented, shrieking screams.*

The cacophony and destruction was immediately followed by eeriest sound–*total silence.* There were no sounds at all. Nature had provided a moment of reverence for the recently departed. No one spoke and the birds no longer sang. It was like the whole world had gone deaf. We had been placed in a vacuum so we could contemplate everything we had just heard and seen. Helicopters must have come. But, there was no rush to evacuate the wounded. There were no wounded, just bodies and parts of bodies.

There was no attack either. That track had happened upon an improvised explosive devise placed in the middle of nowhere.

Obviously, the giant land mine was evidence that the enemy was in the area. Soon the whole company would be coming back and we would be looking for the gooks that planted that mine.

Bandido Charlie was moving in. The Viet Cong *had better* be moving out.

A short time later forty-eight APCs and two M-60 Tiger Tanks cruised through the brush looking for trouble. One of the track commanders detected movement. The entire Company wheeled and turned. The chase was on. Dozens of rubber trees were mowed down as we pursued our elusive prey. We joked that, after we won the war, the United States government was going to have to pay Michelin $10 for each tree we damaged. The target we were chasing managed to keep breaking-off contact and reappearing. For the better part of an hour we chased, lost, and pursued. Finally, it was confirmed. We had been chasing a stag deer.

Deer were just a small part of the diverse wildlife living on the Michelin Rubber Plantation. Huge spiders spun heavy yellow webs between the evenly spaced trees. They waited silently, centered in their colossal traps, ready to ambush birds. A man on foot could pass under one and never know that it was there. However, the super-sized arachnids were suspended at exactly the right height to deposit themselves onto the top of a passing Armored Personnel Carrier.

Ants, the kind that deliver painful bites, built nests made from leaves in the trees. These ant colonies were perfectly camouflaged and positioned in such a way that just brushing past them would spill hundreds of angry little vermin onto unsuspecting GIs. Shaking red ants out of clothing at thirty miles an hour, while suffering their repetitive attack, was entertaining for anyone watching. Entertaining until the one of the nasty little creatures found their way onto those being entertained.

One time, I had an ant crawl up into my ear. The sounds it made while scrounging around inside my head are difficult to describe. Fortunately, it didn't bite me while in my ear.

We never saw any of the tigers reported to be roaming on the plantation. Cobras, on the other hand, were plentiful. They flourished in the elephant grass meadows that separated stands of trees. The cobras appeared as slithering black ribbons gleaming in the wake of flattened grass that marked our APC's passage.

Bandido Charlie met-up with a group of straight leg infantry grunts just outside a grouping of huts in the middle of nowhere. The straight legs had been inserted by helicopter. Before they met-up with us they had been on a walking patrol for at lest a week. They hadn't been resupplied. These guys had been drinking the kind of nasty stuff that results from iodine tablets being placed into a canteen full of rice paddy runoff. We shared our regular water (filtered and treated) with the straight-legs.

Our rendezvous, with the straight-legs, had been planned so we could give them a ride. Two squads on one track made for a crowded deck. However, after walking for a week, these guys looked like they *needed a ride*. These walking infantrymen weren't accustomed to bouncing around on top of a track and, with the crowding, some of our guests were perched too close to the edge. Our first priority became a vigil to keep our guests from being accidentally bumped overboard. The continual growl of our diesel engine wasn't conducive to conversation. Therefore, we really didn't have much of a chance to get to know these Grunts. Just seeing how exhausted they looked made us grateful for not being them.

Late in the afternoon, Charlie Company stopped on the edge of *yet another* sea of eight-foot tall elephant grass. The squad that had been riding with us was let off. They were going on an ambush patrol. Wishing them luck we watched them walk, single file, toward a darkening tree line 150 yards to the west. Once they reached the trees they should have turned, found a concealed position and set up an ambush. Bandido Charlie continued east into the vast flat expansive tropical prairie. Our passage left earth bound contrails of crushed vegetation that dissolved into the lengthening shadows.

The Straight-leg Grunts, on foot a ¼ mile behind us, hadn't reached the trees when we stopped again. This time the tracks closed ranks, almost to the point of touching, and executed a big pinwheel maneuver. Armored Personnel Carriers flattened a huge circle into the tall grass. The two M-60 tanks, mortar squads, command track, and cooks set-up in the center, as usual. Everyone else took equally spaced positions right on the edge of the perimeter. My squad was facing east with the sunset and woods behind us.

Half of our squad began deploying our chain-link fence RPG Shield immediately after we stopped. Post installation was achieved by placing an empty artillery shell casing on top of a long metal fence post and hammering the fence post into the ground using a sledge hammer. The auditory effect was loud without being musical. On a still evening, like this one, the cacophonic effect was the opposite of stealthy. Cliff shouted, above the racket, that we were on Listening Post again.

This time, we were to take one of the new replacements with us. Perez had joined Bandido Charlie only yesterday. He was from

Puerto Rico and hardly spoke English. Cliff and I had done LP many times. Our sergeant knew that Cliff and I worked as a two-man team. He wanted us to show the new guy how it was done.

Perez was mute to the point of being sort of dopey. We figured that, as a still-clean replacement, he was probably just suffering from sleep depravation. Cliff and I checked him out. We made sure that he had a loaded M-16, Claymore mine, complete with detonator, and a poncho to lie on. Cliff and I attributed his near silent compliance to his not speaking much English. Perez might have been overwhelmed, confused by the strangeness of his new surroundings. Cliff and I carried the same equipment with an additional two-way radio and back-up batteries.

Cliff took point, the new guy was in the middle and I followed. We didn't go far from the edge of the perimeter. The dry grass was at least eight feet high and incredibly dense. Walking was like trying to swim, in a vertical position, under water. All the grass stems made it feel like you were going to trip, feet and legs were always tangled. But, falling over would have been impossible. The vegetation was so thick that it wouldn't let you fall down and so dense that a person standing five feet away would have been totally invisible.

Walking in this very tightly packed grass was walking blind—it was total sensual deprivation. Nonexistent visibility, muted sound and entangling stems combined to give the sensation of being buried. The impenetrable grass towered over our heads. A small window open onto the sky was formed where we trampled a place to lie down. Our small window to the sky gradually changed from dark blue to black. The claustrophobic effect was like being buried in a haystack. The only sense that worked was smell and the only smell was grass. The tightly packed foliage even muffled the sounds of Bandido Charlie behind us.

Our role, as an early warning for the company behind us, was questionable at best. Usually, we would find a concealed place to watch and listen for the enemy. Under these conditions, we couldn't see or hear anything. An enemy could pass just a few feet on either side of our position without our knowing. Someone would have to trip over us before we would know that they were there. We were a Listening Post that was simultaneously deaf and blind.

Nonetheless, we flattened a circle in the grass, hoping that we wouldn't stomp on a sleeping cobra, and spread out our poncho liners. The starless sky formed a black roof over the stem-lined walls of our Listening Post. The only view was straight up—it was like looking up from inside a well or from the bottom of a round grave.

Each of us trailed the detonator wire for a Claymore mine behind us and used it as guide to find his way back to our Listening Post position. The Claymore's electric detonator cord was a wire that looked like any ordinary household extension cord. The mines we set formed an arched defense 50 feet in front of our position. A Claymore mine is an explosive device made with marble sized steel balls embedded in C4 plastic explosive. Packaged in a curved gray plastic case, the mine was detonated with a blasting cap. This gadget is considerably more powerful than a hand grenade. It could also be rigged as a booby trap with a trip wire. These mines were supposed to be exploded as we were leaving our position *after* reporting approaching enemy. Under those conditions it wouldn't be prudent to spend a lot of time searching, in the dark, for the detonators. Cliff and I tethered our mines' detonator wires to the radio's shoulder straps. Perez didn't want to part with his detonator and assured us that he would keep it within reach. Placing the radio in a central location was the final touch that completed the preparation of our sensory-deprived Listening Post.

In hushed tones, we explained to Perez that the only time he was to speak was into the radio and that was only when he had actually seen or heard enemy movement. We whispered out of habit. Charlie (Viet Cong) wouldn't have been able to hear us anymore than we could have heard him. Still, we kept the radio's volume really low. Any inquires from the command post would be answered by breaking squelch (keying the microphone to make a static sound).

Since he looked exhausted, Perez was to have the first watch. Cliff thought that, if Perez went first, he would be able to catch two straight hours of sleep after his turn. Then, he would be more alert for his second watch. Cliff was wrong.

The thick layer of grass under the heavy rubber of our ponchos formed an incredibly soft mattress like padding. I was asleep, loaded M-16 (safety off) at my side, in an instant.

Charlie Company's First Sergeant's face suddenly appeared, suspended upside down, inches from my face. He was rudely shaking me from a sound sleep. I thought that I must still be dreaming. This guy hardly ever talked to me. His face looked nightmarish floating in the darkness. Still, I must be awake because Sarge was using curse words that I could never have dreamt of.

I didn't want to show the evil spirit in this nightmare that I was afraid. So, I tried to put innocent inquiring quality in my question. "Sarge, what are you doing here?" I asked the disembodied apparition (his torso was behind the curtain formed by the grass). I didn't expect an answer.

"Waking up your sorry ass!" answered the angry ghost. ***His*** tone was definitely furious. Somehow he managed to control the volume of his voice. Sarge's stage-whisper barely conceal his rage, "When you dumb sons of bitches didn't answer the radio we figured that you were dead. I came out here to collect your dog tags. If you fall asleep again I won't be coming to get you!" I didn't realize, for sure, that I wasn't dreaming until Cliff confirmed the identity of the Sergeant as he stormed back to the temporary Firebase. I had never seen him so annoyed.

Giving Perez the first watch hadn't worked. He had slept through it, and snored through the Sergeant's little visit as well. In fact, we had to wake him up just to advise him that sleeping on guard was not the usual way of making a good "first impression" on his new commander. We were going to give Perez another chance. This time, *he would get the third watch* and hopefully be rested enough to stay awake when his turn came again.

Cliff and I spent the next two hours watching Perez sleep and whispering to each other about our anticipated visit with the Judge Advocate.

Two hours after Sarge's visit, we shook Perez awake and made sure that he was cognizant. Cliff and I were satisfied that Perez was fully conscious and listening for enemy movement. It had been a long hot day and it was so cool and quiet lying on the soft grass mattress—I was almost instantly asleep again.

A thunderous explosion blasted me awake. Actually, the conflagration was the first in a *rapid series* of extremely loud and very close explosions. **We were under attack!** Orange outgoing and green incoming tracers zipped through the black circle serving as our ceiling/window. Fireflies on steroids were speeding across the night sky delivering messages of death. A booming thump, immediately followed by a whistle—diminishing in both volume and pitch—meant that our mortars were firing. A similar whistle, declining in pitch while increasing in loudness, preceded the even louder explosion announced incoming mortars. Both circumstances were occurring simultaneously. I had awakened from a dreamless sleep into a real nightmare.

We had to get back into the perimeter!

First, I had to tackle Perez. He had started to run in a direction that would have taken him away from the tracks. "We have to call in," Cliff shouted above the chaos. "We gotta let 'em know that we're comin' or we'll be shot as soon as we step out of the grass!" Stealth was no longer a consideration. Radio traffic was heavy at the moment. We had to wait for a break in the chatter before we could announce our impending return. It seemed as though a break in radio traffic would never come.

Cliff and I used those moments to find our detonators and set-off our Claymore mines. Perez couldn't find his detonator, *just one more reason to want to kill this guy*. We were crawling on our hands and knees in pitch-black darkness trying to retrieve that last detonator. We finally found it and set off Perez's mine.

Blowing our mines had gotten the attention of the Commander's radioman. We no longer had to wait to use the radio. We assured Captain Goldberg that we were indeed alive and ready to come back into the perimeter. Apparently, they had been trying to reach us for some time and had given us up for dead...*a second time*.

Released from the claustrophobic confinement of our Listening Post, we saw the scale of the battle raging around us. The main body of the attack was coming from the north. Our Mortar Platoon was firing flares illuminating the Firebase, as well as dropping rounds on the enemy. The Defensive Concentrations (Def Cons) exploding around our perimeter were coming from the big Howitzers at Lai Khe. They were also zeroing in on the enemy positions. Helicopter gun ships, circling directly overhead, rained fire from above. The gunships flew without navigation lights. The Cobra gunships were invisible until their mini-guns sent laser-like strings of tracer bullets down from the pitch black sky. An inner perimeter had formed between the tracks anticipating the enemy breaking out of the wall of grass. Any attempt to over run our position would surely mean close-quarter combat.

The tension was palpable as we waited for the bad guys to show up. Noise and smoke filled the night. Flares, trailing smoke as they swung on slowly descending parachutes, produced deep moving shadows. Harsh glaring light from the burning white phosphorus flares illuminated the interior of the Firebase. The curtain of grass in front us could open at any moment admitting hordes of screaming enemy troops.

Our track was facing east, away from most of the action. The 50-caliber machine gunner didn't have steady work, he fired intermittent bursts at anything he perceived as movement.

"Who's helping our gunner? You know, passing him ammo and helping him spot movement and stuff," I asked a silhouetted Cliff. The flare-light made near black shadows totally lacking in detail.

Cliff just shrugged an "I don't know" reply. He probably thought that I wouldn't have heard him with all the racket.

Figuring that the gunner could use some back up, I climbed the rungs on the trailing face of our Armored Personnel Carrier, crawled over the litter covering the deck and tapped the gunner on his shoulder. He jumped. Apparently, he was a little jittery.

"What in the hell are you doing up here!" he shouted over the pandemonium of the artillery barrage.

"Just wanted to see if you needed anything." I yelled back. "How are you fixed for ammo? You want some water or anything?"

There was a pause in the shooting. He replied, in a calmer almost casual voice "Naw, I'm OK."

Taking advantage of the relative quiet I asked, "How's it goin'?"

"It's not so bad on this side of the perimeter. Charlie's over there." He said pointing to his left while keeping his eyes on his field of fire. "They're about a half mile away. You can see the flash from their mortars. Our artillery is zeroing in on 'em. We're blowin''em into dust." He said with a grim smile that was barely visible in the flickering light of the aerial flares. A neighboring 50-caliber opened up sending red-hot tracers into the grass 100 feet out and slightly to our left.

"You want me to hang out and give you a hand?" I asked.

"Naw, I got everything that I need close by," he replied.

"Well, just give a holler if you need anything," I said before turning to go.

Standing erect, I looked for those enemy mortar flashes to the north. Instead my attention was distracted by another firefight directly behind our APC a quarter-mile to the west. The commotion in the tree line at about the same place where the straight-legs would have been if they hadn't turned and sought better concealment. It was one hell of a fight. Tracers were going everywhere. I wasn't able to watch for very long before something, even closer, caught my eye.

A Cobra Gun Ship, hovering directly overhead, was firing its mini-gun at a target directly in front of the track I was standing on. The helicopter gunner must have been shot. His aim abruptly fell short and he put quite a few rounds inside our perimeter. Before the gunship stopped shooting, the incoming bullets made a sound like individual links from a chain falling to the ground in rapid succession. I imagined a chain hanging, like a rope, that had been released from some great height as the chopper pulled away. The orderly series of small, evenly spaced thuds, were no further than ten feet away to my right. The sound began at the edge of the perimeter, and continued between the tracks into a line of Grunts. A GI I had been standing next to only minutes before crumpled to the ground. One moment he was standing there, part of the interior perimeter guard–an instant later he was a heap on the ground.

On hands and knees, I searched for a first aid kit hidden in the harsh shadows from the flares overhead. It should have been buried somewhere in the litter on top of the track. I rummaged through the poncho liners, flack jackets, multiple M-16s and ammo. I never did find it. Pausing in my search, I saw that a medic was already working on the wounded guy. Apparently, the combination of his standing and the angle of the incoming round had caused a single bullet to enter high on the back of the guy's right shoulder. It exited just under his collarbone without causing serious damage. He was wounded, but alive, and would be medi-vaced out on the next chopper.

I jumped down from the track's deck with one of the M-16s. My pockets now filled with M-16 ammo clips and a cardboard box with medical first aid dressing. I took a position standing with everyone else. We were just standing there, watching the fighting and waiting to for the enemy to come out of the tall grass.

The unmistakable sound of diesel engines firing-up was suddenly added to the noise of combat. Some tracks, on the southern edge of the perimeter, were preparing to go somewhere. The Company 1st Sergeant, who had been so uncharitable only moments ago, was talking to small groups of Grunts behind the idling tracks. I went over to him. He was looking for volunteers, and having varying degrees of success. Sarge was forming rescue party to retrieve the straight leg ambush patrol that I had watched, as it was being ambushed.

"Poris and I will volunteer to go and get those Grunts for you Sarge," I said. "All we ask is for you forget about that little incident concerning our sleeping on Listening Post."

"Sure, asshole. Get your partner over there before those tracks leave, and you have a deal." He wheeled and turned looking for more volunteers.

I found Cliff with the guys bandaging up the Grunt who had been shot near our track.

"Come on Cliff, I volunteered us to go rescue some straight legs." I said pulling him in the direction of the idling APCs on the southern perimeter.

"Are you nuts? Charlie is all over the place. He could be anywhere." A certain lack of enthusiasm was evident in his response.

"You don't understand," conjuring my powers of persuasion. " We do this and we're off the hook for Perez sleepin' on LP. Either we go out there and bring back those Grunts or we spend the rest of our tour in LBJ (Long Binh Jail). There isn't a lot of time for you to think about this. We gotta go. Beside, if you were able to volunteer us for that lousy Recon Patrol, I can volunteer us to go on a little midnight ride."

Cliff was still holding the loaded M-16 from the Listening Post debacle. We ran toward the two APCs designated for the rescue and climbed on board. Charlie Company's second in command Lieutenant was topside standing next to the 50-caliber. He had just started explaining that he would be shooting off hand flares every two minutes. His signals would mark our progress and keep us from being shot by our own helicopters. Everyone listening was genuinely impressed. We all had volunteered to be placed in a potential crossfire. We could become targets for the enemy, as well as our own gunships.

With the cheerful possibility of becoming victims of "friendly fire," we headed out to rescue the shot-up patrol.

In a cool display of courage while not under fire, the Lieutenant marked our passage by nervously firing hand-held flares as rapidly as they were handed to him. The men crowded on top of the moving APCs, silently watched the Lieutenant's one-man pyrotechnic display. Should we have just sent arrival announcements? After all, he was giving the enemy regularly updated reports on our progress.

Our mad dash across the field of elephant grass ended at the tree line without incidence. Both growling diesel engines simultaneously dropped their noise level to a barely audible murmur. The two APC engines were almost synchronized to the point of making a pulsing and throbbing sound, like huge beasts catching their breath after a long run. The pandemonium from the battle raging at the Firebase seemed strangely distant. A spooky quiet settled on the rescue party. Big artillery flares eerily lit the trees. *No one spoke.* The slowly descending illumination caused irregular shadows to march upward, in unison, on the trees. Massive tree trunks formed a solid outer wall of densely foreboding jungle. The moving glare of the flare light only illuminated the first row of looming trees. The creeping light didn't penetrate into the forest. The immense trees appeared to be an unyielding black barrier. The ambush patrol had vanished, somehow the trees devoured it. The patrol had simply disappeared. Had the drivers found the right spot?

All eyes searched the impenetrable blackness beyond the massive wall of trees. The rescue party had become motionless targets silhouetted by flare-light. We had seen the straight leg ambush patrol being attacked. Was it our turn? Another attack seemed imminent. Tension paralyzed the Lieutenant. Thankfully, his barrage of Roman Candles flares had stopped. The black barricade of trees revealed nothing. One thing was certain…*whatever came out of those trees would not be good.*

A barely perceptible moan drifted over the idling engines.

A weak disembodied voice whispered, "We're over here." Almost immediately, more voices chimed-in, simultaneously expressing pain and need. We had come to the right place.

Strangely enough, the men on the tracks maintained an unordered silence. Our makeshift band had been formed in a hurry. We hadn't been briefed on exactly what we were to do once we had arrived. Anticipating a firefight, no one was anxious to exchange the familiar armed-to-the-teeth APCs, for the frightening unknown darkness. No one wanted to put down their weapons and be caught in a potential crossfire while helping the wounded. Everyone waited for orders. A seeming eternity passed while the rescuers ignored the escalating sounds of pain and pleading from the men in the woods. No one moved. We were all paralyzed.

One guy, 'Doc' the medic, jumped off of the track closest to the woods. He crashed into the trees. Doc disappeared into the darkness carrying only a bag of medical supplies and a stretcher. Doc had no weapon.

"Come on you guys, I need some help!" he shouted from the darkness. "I need a hand with the other end of this stretcher."

Still, no one moved.

Figuring that *somebody* had to go, I silently volunteered (for the second time in less than an hour) by jumping from the APC. I couldn't carry both a wounded guy and an M-16. So, I left my weapon behind. I followed the sound of Doc's voice. Thrashing around in the void-like gloom, Doc and I unfolded the stretcher. The medic hefted an unresponsive GI onto the canvas litter. I grabbed a pair of handles and lifted on Doc's command. We stumbled back to the waiting tracks.

Doc yelled to the driver, "Drop the damn gate! This guy is heavy."

No one had moved off of the Armored Personnel Carriers. At this rate, the rescue was going to take some time. The good news: if we hadn't been shot at by now we probably weren't going to be shot. Maybe the bad guys didn't want to mess with the APC's firepower. Or, they had just left.

The gate slowly opened. While it was still six inches off the ground I stepped up onto the ramp. It was just as dark inside the track as it had been back in the woods. The driver refused to turn on even the red 'black-out' interior lights. After I was past the ramp, formed by the lowered gate, it was easier to crawl into the pitch-blackness. I set down my end of the litter, cleared a space for the stretcher and pulled the guy in while scooting backward on my knees. It took even more time to navigate my way out. After all, I didn't want to step on the stretcher guy.

Doc had collected another litter and headed back into the trees for our next customer. I followed him.

"How many more do we have to carry out Doc?"

"Two to carry, the rest should be able to walk, with some help." He answered.

"Hope that you can see where we're goin'. My eyes just aren't adjusting to the dark."

"Follow me." was his only reply.

Image by Tony Hallas

As I was going up the ramp with the second stretcher I asked, "Where are we gonna put 'em Doc? I don't think the seats are wide enough to hold a stretcher and the first guy is kinda takin' up all the room in the center."

"Just put him on top of the first one." Doc said flatly.

"Come on Doc, isn't he hurt bad enough already?" I protested.

"He won't feel it." Doc answered.

Until that moment I didn't know that we were loading dead bodies into the APC. The third one was placed on top of the other two. Their bodies formed an unstable pile in the middle of the track. It was a teetering heap ready to fall over at any moment. We left them and went back after the injured Grunts.

The wounded were badly hurt. We carried/dragged them, in a more or less vertical position, to the canvas bench seats that lined the Armored Personnel Carrier's interior walls. The less severely wounded hobbled to the track, arm-in-arm. Doc used a fireman's carry for the guys who couldn't walk. He reassured the wounded soothing them, telling them that they were *going to be all right* as we walked them out of the darkness. Doc and I made several trips back into the trees. We assisted the wounded any way we could, supporting as they hobbled up the ramp into the track. None would have made it into the track under their own steam.

The rescue party maintained their silent vigil, standing guard concentrating on the darkness between the trees. Listening, as well as watching, for movement. Thirty fingers on thirty hair triggers were waiting to go off. Even the cries of pain from the wounded stopped. Grim determination took hold of the rescue effort. Everyone was going back to the Firebase.

Doc and I quickly checked the area to make absolutely certain that we left no one or any equipment behind. We watched the tailgate close. As Doc and I climbed on board, I remarked about how spooky it must be for those wounded Grunts. They were sealed inside a totally dark APC with their three dead friends.

The Armored Personnel Carriers sped back to the battle at the Firebase. The Lieutenant only fired off two flares during the whole trip back.

The returning APCs resumed their out-facing positions on the perimeter and the volunteers scrambled off. I joined a small group watching the tailgate of the track I had just loaded. The ramp slowly lowered into its open position. The flare light seemed much brighter here. The red lights were turned on inside the track. Wounded Grunts squinted out of the APC's interior. Red interior lights, reflecting off red blood, made the liquid look like shiny black pools. In the eerie crimson glow the wounded looked like ghosts spit back from hell. The rescued men didn't say much. They had been sitting in near total darkness while being pitched about on, and probably off, narrow canvas seats during their ride to our perimeter. In unimaginable physical pain, these infantrymen had sat inches away from the bodies of their dead comrades. Shock, hurt and fatigue was etched onto their faces. Their numb silence was testimony to their suffering. Inside the relative safety of the perimeter, there were plenty of other people to help. I went back to my squad to wait for the attack.

The fighting stopped as suddenly as it began. The enemy simply stopped shooting. The incoming mortars stopped. Eventually we stopped, too.

The battle's pandemonium was replaced by creepy silence. For a while, the artillery flares kept coming. That was when I noticed that flares make a peculiar spooky sound. A loud pop (nothing like an explosion, more like a distant firecracker) would precede a glaring bright light in the inky night sky. The magnesium flare trailed copious amounts of smoke as it slowly swung beneath a white nylon parachute. A bizarre whooping sound would accompany each flare. The sound had a faint and peculiar echo. It was a low oscillating noise, like a distant loon on a far away lake. This strange reverberation was made by the can portion of the artillery flare. The same small charge, that ignited the flare, also popped the lid off of the flare's containment canister. That falling can would spin, as it fell, and make a strange low noise, like someone blowing over the edge of a very large bottle. The flares eventually stopped, silence re-enforced the darkness.

Everyone knew the enemy was out there. There was no need for Listening Posts. Everyone was awake. We just *hurried-up and waited*, watching the tall wall of grass that surrounded us.

Eventually our patient anticipation was rewarded with another spectacular sunrise in paradise.

More medi-vac or Dust-off choppers came with the first light. The remaining wounded went to the hospital in Lai Khe. A second wave of resupply helicopters immediately followed, leaving ammunition and taking the dead. Before they left, I went to pay my respect to the guys who were dealt out of the game last night. They no longer had to *hurry-up to wait.* They were lined-up, in an orderly row, under green plastic ponchos; only their boots were showing. There were more than the three our rescue party had picked up last night, maybe a dozen altogether.

The tracks we used for last night's rescue mission were parked where we had left them. Their rear gates were still open. Warm morning sun revealed carnage inside of the one track that had actually carried the rescued. Its floor was a jumble of sandbags and equipment. Blood spatter was everywhere. Red pools had formed on the floor between the sandbags. A thick red mixture of dust and congealing blood slowly oozed out onto the ground.

When I got back to the squad, Cliff said that the cooks hadn't made breakfast. That meant two things: 1) if there was any eating to be done it would come out of a can (C-ration breakfast is easy to pass up) and 2) we would be moving-out. There wasn't even coffee. We were going to be leaving, real soon.

We were heading into the jungle. At one time it may have been the Michelin Rubber Plantation, it was jungle now. Bandido Charlie went directly to the location where last night's enemy mortar fire had originated. There were dead enemy bodies and blood trails leading off in all directions. Apparently, we had gotten some of them too.

In a war zone dead bodies are not all that uncommon. After all, it is a war zone. We always just left the enemy dead to rot. Jokes weren't appropriate. After all, *but for the grace of God...* Occasionally someone would make a comment about a corpse. But, generally speaking, our observations were more *forensic*. We commented about what had actually killed a dead gook. Do you think he was decapitated before he had that big hole in his side?

We motored past one memorable Vietnamese corpse. He was laying spread eagle in the elephant grass. He was on his back right in the center of a spot where an artillery shell had blown the grass flat. This corpse was centered in the middle of a fairly large circle with all the long tan blades radiating away from a relatively small crater. This particular corpse was unusually pristine. He was centered on the spot where an explosive shell had detonated. Lying there, with his eyes closed, the setting was so artistic that it looked intentionally posed. There wasn't a mark on him-no blood, no missing parts. This Viet Cong looked like he was sleeping. Anyone who had been standing that close to an explosion should have been more than just dead. He should have been a bloody stained spot on the ground. Battlefield bodies just never look *restive*. They're horrific; often torn to bits.

For some reason, this scene just didn't look *right*. As we slowly motored past this impeccable cadaver, it occurred to me that he was faking. I considered pumping a few rounds into him-j*ust to call his bluff*. But, then decided against it. The column of tracks would have had to stop and somebody would have to find out why I shot a corpse.

We moved on. So what if one got away?

We'll catch him next time.

RE-DEAL

South of Lai Khe the terrain changed. North of the division basecamp, cultivated rice paddies lined the road. Now, we were definitely more 'off-road,' in a less populated area with much heavier vegetation. There were more trees and not just rubber trees. After the attack in the elephant grass, we moved into a natural clearing in the jungle and built a new Firebase from scratch. It was a considerable distance away from roads and people. The usual Vietnamese camp followers were unable to catch-up with us. We were in the middle of nowhere. The new firebase must have had a name, but like so many other Firebases, I never knew what it was called.

One bright morning, as our new encampment neared completion, Captain Goldberg summoned me to the Command Center. I hoped that he didn't want to discuss that incident with Perez falling asleep on Listening Post.

"I see that you have a secondary MOS as a correspondent. Is that right?" he asked.

I was caught totally off guard and relieved at the same time. I couldn't help but wonder where this unexpected line of questioning was going. It was surprising that the Captain had read my personnel file at all, much less in such detail. As I answered the Captain's question, I realized that I had almost forgotten about *what now seemed like* a useless footnote on my service record.

"Well, there is an opening back at Division, in Lai Khe. The Public Information Office needs a photographer. Do you think that you could handle the job?"

I stammered an affirmation, saying that I thought that I could handle such a job.

"I think so, too. There is a Chinook leaving here in a half hour. Get your stuff together and be on that chopper. You have done a good job. Get outta here and I don't want to see you back without a camera. Good luck." The Captain reached out and shook my hand.

I stumbled back to the track stunned and almost in shock. The comprehension of what had just happened hadn't really sunk in.

My life, as a Grunt, had just been dramatically changed.

The fact that I might no longer be a dog-faced ground pounder was amazing beyond my sleep-deprived imagination. But, what would happen to Cliff? Who was going to watch his back and keep him from getting shot? We had watched-out for each other for the last three months. How could I just walk away from such a good friend? As I walked back to my squad's track I was wracked with concern to the point of guilt. Our bond was like family. The thought of leaving my friend and *brother* plus the guys we had risked our lives with somehow didn't feel quite right. I felt guilty for my good fortune.

I told Cliff about going back to apply for a new job. He broke into a big grin. " You lucky son of a bitch. *You're gonna be a REMF!*"

"A REMF?"

"Yeah, a **REAR ECHELON MOTHER FUCKER!**" He kept laughing and slapping me on the back. Cliff was *actually* happy about my leaving. His jubilation surprised me and relieved me from my guilt. I knew that I would miss him.

Packing didn't take long. My personal belongings fit into my pockets. I promised Cliff that I would keep in touch. I kept my concerns about Cliff's welfare to myself and left.

I was going on my first helicopter ride.

The first of many helicopter rides to come.

REMF

Evidently, I made a bad 'first impression' on Sergeant First Class Stevenson. He sent me away. Sargeant First Class Stevenson was the non-com office manager for the First Infantry Division Public Information Office (PIO). I stood before his desk and explained that I was responding to an advertisement in the *Stars and Stripes*. As far as Stevenson was concerned, I was a dogface private who was lost and had somehow wandered into his office. I had no appointment and my uniform did not meet Headquarters Company standards. The fatigue shirt I was wearing didn't have a nametag sewn on it. There was no 'Big Red One' patch on my left shoulder. My boots were not shiny enough and I needed a haircut.

Stevenson did not know, or care, about Captain Goldberg (Charlie Company's Commanding Officer and the person who had sent me to the PIO) or me. The only thing Sergeant First Class Stevenson claimed to have any knowledge of was the ad for a photographer. Sergeant Stevenson suggested that I leave, get my uniform in order and try again.

While I was still standing in front of Sergeant First Class Stevenson, I thought that I should have made a list of his observations. He had suggested that I do so many things before I returned. I didn't want Sergeant First Class Stevenson to repeat his list of of my personal shortcomings. I was in a hurry, but, I also didn't want someone else to get the job. I had taken a shower that morning; the third one in three months, this obviously was not good enough. Sergeant First Class Stevenson expected me to be more than simply clean. He wanted me to smell like a FNG (fucking new guy) replacement. My shirt was almost new. Sergeant First Class Stevenson was correct, my shirt only had 'U.S.ARMY' embroidered on a patch over my upper left pocket, and it had no nametag or division insignia. I was shaved.

My fatigue pants were clean and almost the right size. They didn't have holes, bullet or otherwise. Was Sergeant First Class Stevenson actually expecting that my shirt and pants to be *pressed*, as in not wrinkled? There wasn't much I could do about Sergeant First Class Stevenson's list of criticisms while just standing there. I had to get moving. However, there was one thing on his list that I could do before I left: make an appointment.

My meeting with Major Chick was set for the following afternoon. As I was leaving the office, I turned and asked Sergeant First Class Stevenson about finding a place to have my haircut. He directed me to a barbershop only one block away. Sergeant First Class Stevenson said it would cost a buck. The Sergeant also said that there was a souvenir shop, right next to the barbershop. They would sell me the patches I needed and sew them on while I waited. I thanked him and left.

I was smitten with the Vietnamese barber from the first moment I laid eyes on her. I tried to avoid staring at her as I sat waiting to have my haircut. She was genuinely beautiful, the first really pretty girl I had seen in months. There are some generalities that could be made about most Vietnamese women, they all said their name was Mai and they all wore either one of two outfits. It was like there was some kind of uniform code. One outfit consisted of a loose fitting pair of black slacks with a white shirt. Both items were made from silky, or at least satin, fabric. The second outfit had the same loose fitting black slacks, but they were worn under a floor length shirtwaist dress. It always had a form fitting on top, with a high Roman collar, many buttons down the front and loose on the bottom with waist high silts on either side. Vietnamese hair, men and women, was always thick, poker straight, and black. Women brushed their hair to a silken sheen and wore it long, usually without bangs. Men always looked like someone put a bowl on their head and cut their hair around its edges. My soon-to-be-barber had those stereotypical features and was still the most uniquely beautiful girl on the entire base. I could have happily spent the entire afternoon watching her while waiting for my haircut. But I was on a mission. I had to get back to my company area. I needed some new clothes, a fresh uniform that hadn't been laundered so many times. If I was going to spend my money having patches sewn onto my shirt, I wanted to start-out with a better shirt. First, I had to get this haircut over with so I could get back to the gift shop before it closed.

I was early for my appointment the next day. I looked better, but I still wasn't prepared. Captain Goldberg had told me that there was a position available for a photographer. I was following his orders reporting for the job. To me, getting the job should have been as simple as showing-up for any other work detail. I thought that all I had to do was flash my secondary MOS. In reality, it wasn't that simple.

Major Chick wasn't impressed with my MOS. He explained that he had run the ad in The **Stars And Stripes**. But, Major Chick had never met or heard of Captain Goldberg (my only *local* reference) and had no idea who he was. So Goldberg's alleged verbal referral was useless and my secondary MOS meant nothing because I had no evidence of actual experience. Major Chick wanted to see what I had done. He wanted to see samples. Where was my portfolio?

I had squat and was on the verge of being sent back to Bandido Charlie.

Major Chick said there wasn't much he could do if I didn't have something–*anything*–to show him. He simply wanted the best man to fill the open position on his staff. I explained how my father had been a teacher and taught photography. How I had worked in the family part-time photography business since I was ten years old, practically growing-up in a darkroom, and how my familiarity with all types of still photo equipment. The Casual Company, back at Ft. Benning hadn't noted on my record that I had worked in the base Photo Lab. All that was just talk. Chick wanted to see pictures. I was about to be thrown out of the office.

I might have to just mark-up this entire interview as being *too good to be true*.

Sergeant First Class Stevenson had been sitting in Major Chick's office, quietly listening, through the entire interview. He finally spoke and offered an alternate possibility—**a fix**. Sergeant First Class Stevenson suggested that Jay Smith, the Specialist in charge of the photo lab, might have a camera that he could let me use. Perhaps I could borrow it. I could use Jay's camera while I was tested over

The Barber, her shop shared the building with the Gift Shop.

a short period of time, say a week. If I didn't work out, in a week, I would be sent back to my unit in the field.

"OK." Major Chick, warming to his assistant's suggestion said, "I'll give you one week. Go see Smith, borrow a camera, take some pictures and have them published in The *Stars and Stripes*. You have seven days. Either you have some pictures published in the *Stars and Stripes* or you'll go back to the boonies with your M-60 machine gun.

I was on my way out when the Major stopped me and added, "Just one more thing: ***Don't bring back any pictures of dead, dirty or wounded GIs.***"

Jay Smith did have a camera, it was a Yashica twin-lens reflex. Smith had purchased the Yashica, during his R&R trip to Japan; it was an imitation of the German Rolleicord. My father had a Rollei, so I was already familiar with holding it and loading film into this awkwardly boxy camera. Like the Rolleicord, the Yashica featured a waist-level viewfinder. The biggest difference between the Rolleicord was its shutter speed control and lens aperture settings being located on opposite sides from where I was used to. Jay's camera used the same size film as my father's camera and produced 2 ¼" square negatives just like the Rolleicord. He would let me use it and even gave me some film.

I spent two days just hanging out around the Public Information Office. For some reason I didn't feel pressured. Not being a target might have lent to my relaxed mood. I was cleaner than I'd been in months and slept inside a tent on a cot. Both of those were big improvements over sleeping on the ground with my shoes on—as I had for the last three months. It felt like I had all the time in the world so I visited with the guys in the office and shot some film. Jay's camera was brand new and worked perfectly. My main objective was to get the feel for the laboratory's equipment and its improvised set-up.

Photo labs require a lot of water. Photographic prints and film are processed in liquid chemistry. Photo chemicals come as dry powders, are mixed with clean water and work at specific temperatures. A chemical developer is the first step that process. Slightly different developers are used to make images on film and paper. Developer has to be washed off or chemically neutralized. Until the development process has been completed, negatives and film are sensitive to light and have to be handled under very specifically controlled lighting conditions. That's how a photo laboratory name was shortened to "darkroom." Still another chemical "fix" allowed images, on both negatives and prints, to be exposed to light. All of these chemicals have to be cleaned off before the prints and negatives can be dried and used. These chemical processes are temperature sensitive, meaning that the chemistry and wash water is supposed to be roughly "room temperature." Vietnam is located in a tropical climate, without air conditioning, there is only one room temperature: **TOO DAMN HOT.**

An awards presentation.

Our Photo Lab's water came from an eighty-gallon tank outside of a galvanized sheet metal building. The Lab had been constructed in one small corner of a large empty warehouse. At one time the building had been used to store raw rubber. The same water truck that filled the Headquarters Company showers, topped-off our lab's tank nearly everyday. The water was non-potable (not drinkable). Since the tank was outside, the water in the tank was the same temperature as the ambient air. The air temperature in Vietnam ranged from the mid-80s to 110 degrees. That wasn't too bad for the showers, it was way too warm for our photo lab. Inside, the PIO Photo Lab itself was one of a half dozen air-conditioned spaces in Lai Khe. The room was cool, the water was not. So, even with air conditioning, the Photo Lab's heat problem was only *partly* alleviated. However, hot water was not the only problem.

My larger, and more immediate, difficulty centered on some pictures that had to be published in the *Stars and Stripes*. I didn't have a clue about making that happen. How was I to know what editors, whom

I never met, wanted published? The people around the office were friendly—but, they weren't much help. They didn't know precisely what kind of pictures would have to be taken for publication. These guys were writers and audio correspondents. Apparently, everyone did their individual jobs and submitted their resulting stories to Major Chick. He, and the other officers, sifted through everything before it was sent to The *Stars and Stripes*, in Saigon, for editing. The *Stars and Stripes* would go through everything sent in by all of their sources and publish what they saw fit. It was their weekly paper, not Major Chick's. There just wasn't anyone, locally, to ask what was specifically needed at the *Stars and Stripes*.

Jay, the darkroom wizard, was the Public Information Office staffer closest to being a full-time photographer. He had the technical photographic skills, but, Jay defined his job a lab tech. He preferred limiting his photographic stories to award presentations around headquarters. Jay processed the film sent in from 'stringers' out in the field. These stringers were nameless grunts who happened to have cameras. Usually, Jay's pictures were posed, ceremonial or documentary.

The PIO writers didn't know about photo requirements. The radio correspondents didn't care about the *Stars and Stripes*. They did their own thing. Radio guys interviewed GIs and sent the tapes to United States Armed Forces Vietnam (USAFV) where the tapes would be forwarded to radio stations back home and eventually aired on local radio stations. Radio Correspondents also ran *KLIK*, the Division's pirate radio station. Radio correspondents were more tuned-in to musical tastes than published graphics or stories. The PIO officers escorted civilian correspondents out into the field. The office's one-and-only combat artist, Dennis Lee, didn't know about photo requirements either.

LUCKY HAND

Halfway through my one-week audition period, one of the staff writers mentioned that he was going to visit an orphanage near Di An. The orphanage was located between Di An and Lie Khe in the village of Ben Cat, fairly close to the Big Red One Administration Annex. The Public Information Office had an auxiliary branch office in Di An. A small group of guys from the office, along with Major Spriggs from headquarters, would be visiting the orphanage. Major Spriggs was working on some paper work for the adoption of a little girl. The Major planned to take this little girl home with him at the end of his tour. The enlisted men had some hard candy that they wanted to pass along to the cute little orphans. These guys enjoyed spending time away from work playing with little kids. The orphans were victims of the war, practically forgotten and didn't receive much attention. The writer asked if I wanted to go along for the ride and play with sad little kids. After all, these

poor little children were so cute. It would be fun to play with them. How could I say no? Of course, I decided to go along. Almost as

Two correspondents with five kids. We wanted to bring all of them home with us.

an afterthought, I brought Jay's camera along. There might be something worth photographing.

Our adventure began in the back of a ¾-ton truck and ended at the orphanage an hour later. We were surrounded, by dozens of kids, the moment the truck came to a stop. Children were everywhere. *They were ecstatic.* These enlisted men had visited them before and the kids anticipated their visit. The candy and toys were appreciated and seemed to disappear in an instant. Everyone wrestled, tickled and generally had fun with the children. We were in a place that hadn't seen much fun. It was sort of like home, having a good time playing with little cousins.

Their laughter was therapeutic for everyone involved. It brightened everyone's day…everyone's week.

PFC Gordon Bent and a little girl with her new doll.

Major Chaplain Major Howard Easley with two orphan girls.

Major Richard E. Spriggs and his soon-to-be adopted daughter, Ngo Thi Hoa

Even Major Richard Spriggs jumped in and played with everyone until his little girl arrived. Major Spriggs dropped everything and focused on his family's newest addition. The Major's playtime was cut short by the formalities of the adoption process. Even then, his little girl never left his side. Both he and Ngo Thi spent time with the orphanage officials, filling-out paperwork. I hung out, played with kids and shot three rolls of twelve exposure black and white film.

Major Richard E. Spriggs and Ngo Thi Hoa

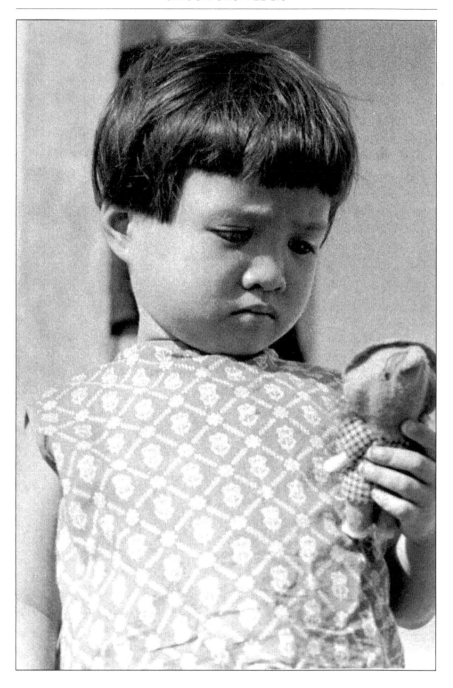

Ngo was four years old and didn't understand why we had to leave her behind

Vietnamese official assisting Major Spriggs with paperwork to adopt Ngo.

That evening, I processed the film. The photos were done the following morning. I wanted Major Spriggs to have some pictures to send home to his family. It was just another exercise for becoming familiar with the new equipment and make some pictures for the Major's family. I made an extra set of prints and submitted them, along with a story one of the correspondents had written for the *Stars and Stripes*. Our stuff made the afternoon deadline.

Stars and Stripes published my pictures and the story about the Major Spriggs. My photos of Ngo Thi Hoa and Major Spriggs were also picked-up by the wire services and published in three stateside newspapers.

I had the job.

The contrast between being a correspondent and a Grunt was the difference between day and night. As a Grunt I had to be *on* 24/7, *on* guard, on alert, I bathed infrequently, ate meals out of little cans, and slept fully clothed wearing my boots. Sleep deprivation provided me the with an ability to sleep sitting upright while holding onto a loaded weapon in broad daylight. I sometimes slept while standing in the chow line.

Sleep deprivation was a timeless dog-face issue. Bill Mauldin, a WWII GI cartoonist, had drawn a sketch with filthy GIs walking down a muddy road. The caption cautioned one guy to not wake Joe up while they were marching. I could identify with that. We slept when we could. We were always tired, always dirty, always hungry or thirsty.

As a member of 1ˢᵗ Administration Company, Headquarters First Infantry Division, everything was 180 degrees opposite. I was only expected to work Monday through Friday from 9-5. I slept in a tent on a cot, covered with a mosquito net. I had a locker and was expected to wear clean clothes and have shined boots every day. I spent $5.00 a month to have  a girl wash my clothes, polish my boots and sweep-out the hooch (Tent where I lived). Hot meals were served three times a day in the mess hall.

I was one of a couple of dozen people–**in the entire Division**–authorized to wear the flashy black 'Official U.S. Army Correspondent' shoulder patch. This emblem was sewn on my left sleeve, over the mandatory Big Red One emblem. I didn't have to wear insignia that designated my rank; in fact, wearing rank was discouraged. This unique situation lead to an innocent deception; we wanted people to believe that we held the highest rank: *civilian*. As far as my job, as a photographer, there was only that one rule. It was that prime directive about ***dead, dirty or wounded GIs***.

There were very few 'assignments.' I was encouraged to creatively *go anywhere* in search of any story. My press pass guaranteed priority travel, on military transport, anywhere on the planet.

I traveled quite a bit and flew enough hours, in combat conditions, to earn an Air Medal.

THOM ARNO

There were rare times when I was sent to cover a specific event. One of those assignments was a story about First Infantry Division soldiers leaving Vietnam to become American citizens. Apparently, the biggest criteria for being drafted into the military service for the United States was simply being in the United States. Personally, I had volunteered for the draft. Many men did not volunteer. They were just drafted. It did not matter whether they were citizens or even born in the U.S. Not only were they inducted into the Army, they were sent to Vietnam. Some of the drafted aliens decided to become citizens. Since they were required to serve in this country's Army, they figured that it might as well be *their* country.

I was part of a three-man team sent to Hawaii, to cover the story of three dozen members of the 1st Infantry Division who were leaving Vietnam to become U.S. citizens. Thom Arno was the reporter and Captain Kelly was a liaison officer from our office. Kelly's wife was living in a rented house on Oahu's north shore. I was supposed to photograph the Naturalization Ceremony. Arno was supposed to write about it. I guess Captain Kelly was supposed to make sure that we came back to Vietnam.

Apparently, an individual could only become a citizen of the United States while they are standing on U.S. soil...*Hawaii was the closest U.S. dirt*. A group of soldiers leaving a combat zone with the objective of becoming citizens was a historic event. I was told that this particular trip was especially *historic* because it was the first time a whole group of GIs had left a combat zone to become Americans.

We had been told that our press credentials were good for first priority military transport part of the trip. We flew to Hawaii on an Air Force Cargo Transport plane: no stewardesses, no soft drinks, one tine toilet and no windows. We sat on seats of cloth webbing that faced backwards. Before we left, I asked about per diem, written orders or some kind of paper work. That kind of thing had always been a requirement for doing anything military. Even a draftee, like me, knew that the Army exists on paper work. I was told that I would only be gone for a couple of days. I was advised to "Take enough money to buy souvenirs and party with. You'll be able eat in mess halls and sleep in a visitor barracks."

We met up with the soon-to-be-citizen soldiers in Di An. Everyone traveled, as a group, to Tan Son Nhut Air Force Base and eventually made it to Hawaii. There was only one overnight stop at Clark Air Force Base in the Philippines. Our Press Passes did function as advertised–they did indeed get us to Hawaii. The problems started after we arrived.

Hawaii has a lot of military bases, all of them claimed that they had no accommodations for a GI traveling on a press pass. This was the first time I had traveled using my press pass. I had not become proficient in the military method for 'proactively' not accepting "no" for an answer. I was in the company of aliens who had no problems finding a place to stay or being fed. They had written orders. I incorrectly rationalized that Thom and my problem arose because we didn't have the proper paperwork and the citizens-to-be did. Our real problem was that we hadn't intimidated the right people.

Finally someone suggested there might be a place for us to stay at Fort De Russy, the Hawaiian R&R center. Married personnel mostly used it. Some of the foreigners were married, so we joined-up with them and headed for downtown Honolulu. The fort was situated right downtown on a beautiful beach. Fort De Russy was a government resort. I didn't see any <u>fort</u>ifications. Fort De Russy was a quiet hideaway with a very good (and inexpensive) bar and restaurant. Thom and I were its only bachelor guests. We even managed to score separate rooms, but we had to pay for them, out of our own pockets with our own money.

Paying for our food and lodging was an unexpected expense. Even with the center's hugely discounted rates (nothing in Hawaii is inexpensive); the meager funds I had allocated for a weekend of partying was gone in no time. Furthermore, the assignment we were told would only take "three-days" stretched-out to last almost ten days. I wound-up borrowing money from the American Red Cross

Miss America and her court. Tom Arno (back center) stands with Judi Anne Ford, Miss America 1969 on his left. Vince Spadafora (center front) is holding my camera, while I watch as Tony Hallas shoot the picture.

to buy food. Still, how could I ask to be reimbursed for the per diem? I left Vietnam to take a 10-day vacation in Hawaii. *Far be it for me to complain about a gig like that!*

My new job title was 'combat photographer.' The Prime Directive wouldn't allow me to emulate my hero David Douglas Duncan. Duncan's Korean War images were, in my opinion, the best war photographs since Mathew Brady's photographs of the Civil War. The prime directive didn't stop me from taking pictures involving dramatic war situations. I did.

I simply sent the film home to my mother. My plan was to make new, and better, prints in my better-equipped darkroom back home. Then, I would use the resulting prints to acquire a job as a civilian correspondent, and come back to Vietnam (at 100 times the salary). Still, there were plenty of stories all over the Big Red One's area of responsibility that would fill my current employer's needs. The orphanage story demonstrated that that Vietnam had a wide variety of heroes.

The Army's defoliating program was best known for its use of Agent Orange. However, there was more than one way to kill vegetation. Rome Plows were effective and didn't get much press. Huge bulldozers were used to knock down wide swaths of jungle. Men operating these machines told exotic tales involving tigers, venomous snakes, land mines and booby traps.

I met one Rome Plow driver who had a run-in with a beehive. He didn't even realize that he had run-over the nest until he was covered with angry swarming bees. His sergeant saw him blindly swatting at the insects as he fell off his plow. The driver was in the process of being stung to death. Having sustained more than 130 stings, this driver was almost unconscious by the time his sergeant reached him. The quick-thinking sergeant saved the Rome Plow operator's life. He grabbed the man covered in angry stinging insects and held him close to his idling Rome Plow's diesel exhaust. The smoke drove the stinging swarm away from both men. The Sergeant returned to work immediately. The driver had a short hospital stay, and went back to work "none the worse for the wear." My photos immortalized him, and his bee's tale in the *Stars and Stripes*.

Rome plow operator and bee victim.

I photographed another story about a GI instructing Army of the Republic of Vietnam (ARVN) troops on the use of WWII Navy landing craft on the Mekong River. The boats took Vietnamese soldiers to fight the enemy in large groups. This particular GI was instructing the ARVNs on the finer points of amphibious assault.

Rome plows clearing the jungle.

He had been hospitalized for nearly two weeks for simply swimming in the Mekong River. An otherwise insignificant scratch went septic after his minor wound came in contact with the river's bacteria laden waters.

There had been a TV show, back home, that had an opening line about a *million stories in the big city*. I took that "million story" concept and applied it to the people all around me.

Everyone had a story to tell.

I interviewed almost everyone I met. Sure, I waded through exaggeration, lies and bullshit. Still, I managed to come-up with enough interesting stories to keep my job. Strangely, clerks told the biggest whoppers, as far as war stories, and the guys who had really been in combat didn't want to talk about it.

I managed to submit plenty of stories without submitting photographs of dead, dirty or wounded GIs. I even kept a clean fatigue shirt, with a First Infantry Division Patch on the left sleeve, in my camera bag. It protected my equipment as well as providing a clean shirt for the occasional GI who may have overstepped the 'dirty' boundary of the *no dead, dirty or wounded* rule.

RICHARD M. NIXON

Bob Hope had visited Vietnam every December during the war. Mr. Hope's many visits were traditional. Richard Nixon came to Vietnam just one time. Nixon was the only president to actually visit Vietnam. *His visit was a really big deal*, to say the least.

President Nixon made an unscheduled five-and-a-half hour visit to Vietnam on July 30, 1969. Nixon had been sworn into his first term in office in January. The Commander in Chief visited South Vietnamese President Nguyen Van Thieu and then came to Di An. President Nixon presented the Distinguished Service Cross to Sgt. Michael J. Murray, 1st Lt. Gary L. Tucker and Captain Enrique P. Rodriguez Nixon completed the awards ceremony and gave a brief speech.

Then, President Richard M. Nixon waded into the crowd of GI spectators. He shook hands with many Big Red One Infantrymen. Civilian photographers and Secret Service members closed in around the President. Everyone crowded-in on this totally unexpected improvised photo op. Tony Hallas and I elbowed our way into the

One of my close-up photographs of Nixon, Secret Service in the background.

President Nixon presented Distinguished Service Cross medals to Sgt. Michael J. Murray, 1ˢᵗ Lt. Gary L. Tucker and Captain Enrique P. Rodriguez

seething mob. I got close enough for several shots and noticed that the President was wearing more make-up than any woman I had ever seen. Tony, who had just finished taking his photographs, said that he wanted to shake Nixon's hand. I told him that I didn't want to touch any guy wearing that much paint and hung back.

Years later, during a 13-part *PBS* Vietnam special, Tony and I were on national television for almost 30 seconds, clowning around and pointing at Nixon from a vantage point on top of an armored personnel carrier.

Dominic Sondy

Tony Hallas shaking
hands with the
Commander-in-Chief

Richard Nixon

Civilian TV crews, filming the event, recorded Hallas and me working
in the crowd and sent Tony this souvenir shot of his memorable
handshake.

An eye-level photo of Nixon working the crowd.

I shot this from the vantage point on top of an APC parked near the ceremonies.

CIVILIANS

Any civilian who spent more than eighteen months in Vietnam, paid no income tax on their earnings. The list of tax-exempt included, but was not limited to, government service employees, civilian contractors, entertainers, and civilian news employees. These people received extra high pay, because of the hazardous conditions, as well as a very healthy per diem.

High tax-free income coupled with that huge per diem and additional vast expense accounts fostered my love/hate relationship with civilian correspondents. They had the world's attention, didn't have to follow the *no dead, dirty or wounded* rule and were paid extremely well. Despite all that, they made us look bad. Fighting a war is hard enough. Having a bunch of critics publicizing our mistakes and prematurely declaring our cause as lost didn't seem right.

The mission of the Public Information Office, as well as my personal goal, was to win the war. The people back home had to be reminded that we were doing the best possible job. Showing *dead, dirty or wounded* would obviously be negative and counter-productive to our purpose. It seemed obvious that our stories had to be favorable about the First Infantry Division.

It appeared that civilian correspondents were paid hundreds of times our salaries, to work against us. Many of these guys were lazy, consistently sloppy or simply put their names on someone else's press release. Think of a hundred Geraldo Rivera's auditioning for the chance to look macho in front of a TV camera.

The major thing that set us apart from our civilians counterparts was our commitment to the troops. Grunts did the heavy lifting. The story of the war was a soldier's story. At the time, I believed that any worthwhile stories about the war should have featured our hard work and sacrifice. Don't get me wrong, the Army is not over-populated with gallant saints. It is like any other group of people. Some are good, some bad. Some are honest. Well, you get the idea. Not everyone was a *hero*. Still, on the whole, a lot of good people were doing their best to defeat an enemy that deserved to be fought.

My civilian counterparts were not always working to illuminate that simple truth.

I had been a Grunt. *I felt obligated to get the infantry's part of the story right.*

My short-term plan was to go out on patrol with the guys and show what a Grunt's life was really like. Sure, most of the time it was a boring life. How does someone photograph sleep-deprived exhaustion? It was more than worth a try. Being in a firefight is hardly ever a planned event. It's usually a matter of being in the right (or wrong) spot at the right moment. Sometimes I was there to capture it on film. Unfortunately, the most dramatic pictures revealed the trauma of the wounded, dying or the dead. Everybody was dirty. Since those images were *off limits*, I carried a clean shirt, with the proper emblems, in my camera bag. That way a GI could change into a clean shirt and pose for the acknowledgment they deserved.

Violating the prime directive would have resulted in my being re-assigned. I wouldn't have been able to tell the GI's story. Sometimes, I simply didn't submit *all of my images*. A certain percentage of my film was developed into negatives (avoiding potential x-ray damage) and sent home. I planned to print my photographs after I got home and produce a quality portfolio. I really wanted to return to Saigon as a civilian correspondent.

I went back to travel with Bandido Charlie. I hung out with straight-legs and patrolled the rice paddies and rivers right on the outskirts of Saigon. I also submitted the "human interest" while sending the dramatic pictures to the one person I trusted–*my mother*. Just trying to print them, much less show them to anyone "in country", would have meant a demotion–at the very least. I went out "into the field" as often as my multiple responsibilities allowed.

My responsibilities at Division Headquarters expanded after Jay Smith finished his tour and had gone home. I spent less time patrolling, more time working on the stringers' stories and handling the logistics that kept the lab running.

Nonetheless, I had accumulated hundreds of images. There would be plenty of high quality images to pick from waiting for me when I got back stateside.

CHRIS NOEL, DIANA DAWN, DONUT DOLLIES AND BOBBIE

Chris Noel proved to be a 1st Infantry Division icon of *morale enhancement.* She was sponsored directly through Armed Forces Vietnam. Chris left a stateside movie career in order to express her appreciation for the GIs. She had no entourage and traveled practically alone. Chris managed to reach even the most remote outposts and found herself in dangerous situations more often than any other *morale enhancer.* Although, stories of Chris visiting GIs during heavy combat are probably exaggerated. Chris truly cared about the fighting men in Vietnam. Her commitment continued after the war as well. (More pictures of Chris are on the pages in the 1986 Chicago Vietnam Veterans Welcome Home Parade section of the book.)

Chris Noel

Bob Hope was famous for having pretty girls in his traveling holiday show. He often remarked that they were there for the purpose of "...reminding the GIs of what they were fighting for." His show passed through Vietnam once annually every year of the war. Hope's concept of reminding soldiers about the girls back home continued past the Christmas season. This method of *morale enhancement* was a major part of the USO's year-around mission. Bob Hope's Show was the largest, and most famous, of the morale raising efforts. The USO wasn't the only organization focused on troop morale, the American Red Cross and Armed Forces Vietnam (AFVN) also provided *morale enhancements*.

The USO offered more entertainment than Bob Hope. Admittedly, most of the entertainers were pretty much scaled-down versions of the Bob Hope's familiar formula for success. Diana Dawn was one of those acts. She became famous, in her own special way. Diana's show was less glitzy, more folksy and smaller than the Hope extravaganza. Still, Diana required logistical support to haul her band, generators, costumes and equipment. This made it impractical for her to visit the more remote firebases. All those extraneous items were a low priority for transport. Diana entertained large numbers of GIs with her songs and PG-rated dance routines at medium and large venues.

Even though entertainment choices were limited and lacked variety. The troops were the definition of a *captive audience*' and gratefully accepted whatever 'entertainment' was provided.

The American Red Cross took a more modest approach toward giving the GI's a brief glimpse of American pulchritude. They employed a small cadre of women often referred to as "Donut Dollies." These brave ladies didn't have an "act" or any particular talent. They traveled fast and logistically light. The Donut Dollies went out *into the field*, served the fighting men coffee and donuts, provided a short flirty glimpse of home and retreated back to the safety of Headquarters. Donut Dollies could turn-up at a camp of almost any size. They were always exposed to as little danger as possible. Their *morale enhancement* role also included visits to field hospitals.

Diana Dawn performing for the troops.

For the first time in the history of warfare, television became a limited part of some REMFs recreational experience in Vietnam. No discussion of morale enhancers would be complete without mentioning 'Bobbie The Weather Girl'. She appeared nightly on Saigon's AFVN TV. The weather was always hot. Anyone else reporting that the temperature was going to be either "hot and dry" or "hot and rainy" would have been boring. Bobbie presented the unsurprising monotony of tropical heat in a way that was sexy and fun to watch. She was almost a parody of a weather-caster. Bobbie would spend her few minutes each night telling her limited audience (field units had no TVs) about repetitive meteorology in a mini-skirt. She ended every show with a coquettish dance, set to Rock & Roll and using the same closing line: *"Have a nice day weather-wise and otherwise."*

Chris Noel

Judy Wilmer, Miss New Jersey, was part of the *beguiling* Miss America entourage that toured Vietnam. (Miss America was pictured earlier, in the segment about Thom Arno.

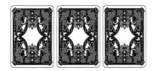

PUBLIC INFORMATION OFFICER

Major **Chick** proved to be unlike another Army officer I had ever met. Besides being an orchestrator, facilitator and humanitarian. Bob Chick proved to be teacher, coach, as well as a mentor.

Major Chick's Public Information Office independently recruited personnel from the Army's vast pool of talented people. The team he built featured writers, photographers and on-air talent. His team's mission was to provide news—news with an optimistic positive bias. We were primarily involved in radio and newspapers. Every member of Chick's staff recognized that their mission was explaining the grim reality of the war as well as telling the people back home about the good positive things we were doing. Despite some civilian reporting, the United States Army was dedicated to seeing the war end successfully. Considering the experience and commitment of our adversary a certain discipline was needed to convey a certainty that we would win.

Major Chick wanted people who had been there. He went out of his way to find men with combat experience. Everyone was dedicated to making it known that American service men and women were doing their best and our sacrifice would not be in vain.

Many people on our team believed that Major Chick saved some lives rescuing experienced warriors from the front lines.

Major Chick's skill at motivating the creative people under his command was not the kind of thing that is taught in a leadership class in Officer Candidate School. Chick was able to mentor his people in an un-military sort of way. He presented abstract problems in a way that enabled his team to create solutions. Perhaps, it was the way he listened to alternatives and encouraged creative solutions.

Major Chick was indeed a most unusual military officer.

Major Vitello became the new Public Information Officer after Major Chick transferred to United States Army Headquarters in Saigon.

Each leader had their individual management style. Both men were extremely good at their jobs. Major Vitello was promoted to Lieutenant Colonel during his tenure at the PIO and was awarded an Army Commendation Medal. Lt. Colonel Vitello's style was *prima class*.

JAY SMITH

Jay Smith, the darkroom technician *extraordinaire*, was discreet. He was principally responsible for the Public Information Office Photo Lab. Jay managed to become my unofficial immediate supervisor and tutor. Smith was the only Specialist Sixth Class (equivalent to a Sergeant E6) that I ever met.

Additionally, Jay was a *short timer;* meaning he was scheduled to go home in a couple of months. His yearlong tour in Vietnam was winding down. I helped to lighten his workload by processing film in the photo lab and, eventually, became his replacement. Unprocessed film came to us from the 'stringers' or the part-timers who submitted their work from the field. Jay would develop the stringer's film, printing *anything* that would produce a recognizable image.

I eventually inherited Jay's lab job, as well as some of his *off of the books* duties.

Jay Smith's receding hairline, combined with his old-fashioned pencil mustache, gave him the look of an "older" man. His demeanor was not quite military. Jay's primary duty was the photo lab. Smith monitored and prioritized the photo lab's workflow while simultaneously scrounging photo supplies (film, chemistry and equipment) without an actual budget. Jay's idiosyncrasies disguised his importance as a member of the Public Information Office team and the 1st Infantry Division. Smith was able to blend into his surroundings. His chameleon's camouflage masked the unusual role he had carved-out in the Division hierarchy.

Specialist Smith also had a *side job* at the Officers Club. Two or three nights a week Jay was paid to operate the Officers Club's movie equipment. He ran a movie projector showing the 1st Infantry Division officers Hollywood's newest releases.

Jay was also responsible for the welfare of Charlie Gibbon–the monkey. Charlie was Jay's pet as well as the PIO's mascot.

As Jay's tour neared its end, Jay shifted all of his responsibilities to me.

Even though I had acquired the PIO photographer's job, the Army didn't have a camera immediately available for my use. I continued to use Jay's Yashica and eventually bought it from him for $30.00. The Yashica was kind of big and clunky for journalistic work. It was new when I borrowed it. But just six weeks of use in Vietnam's heat and humidity turned the inelegant boxy camera into junk. The shutter speed lever and f-stop controls became clogged with fungus. Both controls became inexorably linked and settings would randomly change without warning. Simultaneously focusing, adjusting the lens settings and tripping the shutter was more complex than Chinese arithmetic. The camera became quirky–if not impossible–to use. Three hands were required to make the damned thing work. As much as I liked the Yashica (we had been through a lot) I was forced to junk it.

I was finally issued a Leica. The Leica, a pricey German 35mm camera, was part of a 'kit' that included three lenses and some filters. The Leica proved to be almost indestructible.

It was still in perfect working order when I left the PIO to go stateside.

CHARLIE GIBBON

On slow news days, the monkey Charlie Gibbon provided comic relief in the inherently grim business of war reporting. His photograph accompanied press releases about his career in the United States Army and he was sometimes featured in the 1st Division's bimonthly paper the *American Traveler*. The stories were usually written in the same style that was used when we reported a real person's promotion in rank. Of course, it was all tongue-in-cheek, the writers had fun writing it. We hoped people had fun reading it.

Charlie Gibbon was ultimately given a battlefield commission and was jokingly promoted all the way to the rank of Captain. Of course, our monkey never *really* got a commission, but then again, he wasn't a 'gibbon' monkey either.

In real life, Charlie lived on a leash. His lead was connected to another line that ran, like to a clothesline, from the one time rubber warehouse where, the photo lab had been built, to a backyard bunker. The Public Information Office had been located in a tent when I transferred onto the staff. The building that had been an empty warehouse (except for the photo lab in one corner) sat on a mostly empty lot next to the gift+barber shop. Eventually, the building was totally rehabbed and converted into an office complex. The Public Information Office moved from its tent and into the freshly renovated building where it shared space with the Judge Advocate's Office (JAG) and the American Red Cross.

An above ground-fortified bunker was conveniently located just outside the office's back door. Charlie slept and sheltered from the rain in the bunker. He played outside most of the time except for when he was forced to be holed-up inside the bunker during rocket attacks and foul weather. Charlie had an eerie sense that enabled him to hide in the bunker *before* sirens warned everyone else of an impending rocket attack. Charlie sometimes sat on Jay's shoulder, grooming Jay's sparse hair, as if Jay were another monkey.

Charlie Gibbon was friendly to everyone who learned monkey etiquette. Unfortunately Charlie, like everyone else, treated replacements badly. Initially, the little primate would pretend to be nice to a stranger. The monkey would allow himself to be petted or sit on the new person's head or shoulders. Then, once the new person let his guard down, the monkey would commence a vicious biting and scratching attack or casually stand on the unfamiliar person's shoulder and urinate in their ear. I learned of his tricks the hard way.

I complained to Jay about Charlie's indiscreet rejection of my friendship.

"You have to show him whose boss." Jay explained, "It's pretty black and white with Charlie. Either he is in charge or you are. In Charlie's world, he is allowed to assert his leadership by biting you. If you are in charge, he has to submit to you, allow you to touch him and help you clean yourself by grooming you. *You have to hit him when he bites you.* Otherwise, he will assume that he is boss and keep biting you."

I said that I didn't want to hurt the cute little monkey.

"You can't hurt him. He's tough." Jay said.

I reached out and picked up the monkey. He gave my hand a painful bite.

"Hit him!" Jay encouraged me.

I cuffed the money on the side of his head. He bit down even harder. I hit him again harder still. The monkey went into a rage, screaming, biting and scratching. I lost it.

I lifted the furious ball of fur over my head and threw him, as hard as I could, at the ground. He landed hard and lay motionless just in front of my feet. Charlie had been 'spiked' like a volleyball. I thought I had killed him. Eventually, Charlie sat up, shook himself and climbed onto his new friend's (my) shoulder and tenderly inspected the hair on my head. We were close friends from that moment forward.

Now that we were friends, Charlie might have settled into being a mischievously cute little bundle of gray fur. However, *cute* is in the

Charlie T. Gibbon was friendly to all the staff, but...

eye of the beholder. I suppose that Charlie could be considered *cute* if you could overlook his unusual behavioral quirks.

Charlie had several curiously endearing qualities that combined to make him extraordinary in a kinky sort of way.

Charlie was absolutely fearless, he enjoyed taunting dogs and harbored some additional strange emotional physical appetites.

Charlie would eat almost anything. Everyday, we brought him fruits and vegetables, from the mess hall. He would supplement his *healthy* menu with bugs. He even liked spiders. Some evenings, when the office was empty, we would take him off of his leash and let him run wild inside the office. Charlie would immediately climb into the rafters, capture and eat every spider and lizard.

Vietnamese people, as a rule, do not keep dogs for pets. Therefore, non-military canines were rare. The exception was a small pack of wild dogs that roamed freely inside the First Infantry Division base camp. Seven or eight very mangy looking medium sized mongrel dogs were led by an extremely ill tempered mutt the GIs, in Headquarters Company, had named 'Dumb Shit'. These dogs were not friendly pets. They were vicious scavengers, always looking for food. Anywhere else, these dogs would have been feared in any other community. In this unusual Army neighborhood, most everyone had seen stranger sights than a pack of wild dogs. So, these filthy unloved curs, usually fighting over scraps, were casually ignored.

Charlie Gibbon was not impressed with the mangy mongrels. He was not awed by their fangs or their brutal lifestyle. Astonishingly, our monkey saw these unfortunate cast-off canines as a source of entertainment. He invited the snarling flea-bitten troupe of curs to come into his area Charlie wanted to play. Weighing-in at somewhere between three to five pounds and tethered with a rope, Charlie liked to provoke the wretchedly neglected hounds when ever they ventured near his neighborhood.

Charlie Gibbon had a special, perverse affection for female canines. He got his strange simian kicks by enticing a feminine dog into his area. Charlie would jump up onto her back, grab her tail with both hands, maneuver himself behind her and ride-out his bestial fantasies. The object of his affection invariably made a hasty retreat from his vicinity.

Charlie's amorous escapades would climax when the rapidly departing object of his affection reached the terminus of his leash. The inevitable climax was always premature for Charlie and never soon enough for his unwilling partner.

Male dogs, 'Dumb Shit' in particular, brought-out the sadistic nature of our flyweight mascot. Charlie would coax masculine dogs into his range by standing on the ground. From his apparent point of disadvantage Charlie would intimidate his much larger opponents and challenge them to fight. Charlie used hostile chatter and gestures to bait them. After taunting his unsuspecting victim, goading them to come closer, he would use his patented hop-on-board move to jump up onto the relative safety of the dog's back. Then grab the male dog's tail with one hand. Rather than assault it from the rear,

Charlie would straddle the dog's back. He would use his hand-like feet to enhance his tenacious grip. The monkey would lay face down and backward on a dog's back, hanging onto its sides with his feet and tightly gripping the dog's tail with his hands; while the dog ran in circles, chasing its tail, trying to dislodge him. Gibbon would let go with one hand and reach underneath his opponent. Then, Charlie would apply a vice-like grip to the gyrating dog's genitals. Charlie would hang on tight squeezing the dog's testicles as hard as he could. If the dog tried to shake him off–or worse yet–try to bite him, Charlie would intensify its pain by modifying his hold. Charlie would chomp-down on the base of the dog's tail with his teeth. A snarling threatening dog would instantly become transformed into a pitifully crying, helpless wretch, writhing in torment.

Ultimately the dog would find its way to the end of Charlie's tether and dislodge his torturer. For an instant, while Charlie hung in the empty air behind a rapidly departing dog, a comic look of surprised disbelief would appear on Charlie's face. During that brief second, his monkey face wore the same expression that appears on Wile E. Coyote's face when he discovers that the Roadrunner has tricked him into running off a cliff again. Apparently, Charlie didn't want the pooch to leave while they were having so much fun.

Unfortunately, Charlie Gibbon came to a controversial end. One evening, after dinner, a group of the monkey's human friends found Charles T. Gibbon's lifeless body. He was swinging, with a broken neck at the end of his leash. The spunky little guy dangled, suspended from the lead line between the office back door and the bunker. His fans had brought him some treats. Instead of watching Charlie eat dinner, they speculated about his demise. Some thought it was an accident or a suicide. Charlie was athletic and agile. He had lived on that leash for over a year. Charlie would often tightrope walk on his lead line. He could not have *accidentally* hung himself. Charlie was a lot of things: spunky, brave, perverted, entertaining and endearing. Charlie was not suicidal. Gibbon probably bit the wrong GI and paid with his life. I believe Charlie was murdered.

Charlie was laid to rest behind the office. His funeral was a military affair minus the 21-gun salute. Charles T. Gibbon's obituary noted that he died, *in the line of duty*.

TONY HALLAS

Tony Hallas had been a straight-leg infantry grunt. When he was still out in the boonies, Tony earned a one-day break and was rewarded with a pass. Hallas had seen the same *Stars and Stripes* ad for a photographer that Captain Goldberg had seen. He claimed that he had seen the ad while he was using the *Stars and Stripes* to ignite diesel fuel, while on shit-burning detail. Consequently, instead of using his hard-earned one-day pass for recreation, Tony found his way to Division Headquarters and sought out Major Chick. Tony was a photographer and, unlike me, he actually had a portfolio.

In fact, Hallas' impromptu portfolio was very impressive. It had enough impact to convince the skeptical Major Chick. The Major wanted Tony to join our team. Hallas went back to his unit and explained that he had been presented with an opportunity to transfer to the Public Information Office.

Tony was an excellent photographer. He had been a student at the prestigious Brooks Institute of Photography. Somehow, the Army had decided that Hallas should be a Grunt. Just as I had been my squad's M-60 machine gunner, Tony had become his squad's thump gunner. A "thump gun" is a M-79 grenade launcher. As weapons go, it was not very loud and only produced a rather subdued *thump* sound as it fired a single shot 40mm grenade. Hallas' company commander didn't want Tony to use his powers of observation in the rear as a photographer. Tony's captain wanted to keep Tony walking as the point man for his unit. Hallas' commander had one slight problem.—he was only a Captain. Major Chick, who worked for Division Headquarters, wanted Tony to work for him. As a Major it was easy for him to pull rank and get what he wanted.

That circumstance presented me with the honor of working with Tony Hallas.

Tony transferred into the Public Information Office a couple of weeks after I did. He was more qualified for my job than I was. Initially, I was insecure and feared that Tony would be my replacement. Thankfully, I was wrong. Instead, Tony became my friend. After Jay Smith moved on, Tony and I worked the lab as a team. We developed a friendly competition as far as story submissions were concerned. We also worked, as a team for really big stories, like President Nixon's visit. That way each of us could back-up the other, and make certain that a really important story was totally covered.

My new friend did bring some baggage.

After his dispute, with his former infantry commander (about his transfer to the Public Information Office), Tony was indubitably convinced that the Army was intentionally trying to kill him. He believed that the institution, known as the United States Army, wanted him (personally) dead. On this particular subject Hallas was like the character Yossarian in *Catch 22*. He was paranoid and it was impossible to reason with him about it. After all, we were in the Army and, *the Army* was getting thousands of guys killed. This was what the Army did. Killing people is their business. How can

Tony Hallas after one week in the field.

Photo by Tony Hallas

you not be paranoid when you have witnessed soldiers dying all around you?

Additionally, Hallas was insecure about his stateside girlfriend. She was treating him badly. Tony obviously loved her and she used his affection to manipulate him. I didn't have much to say about his girlfriend. He knew her and I didn't. I just had to listen to him. Why didn't he just dump her? She obviously wasn't worth all of the effort Tony was investing in trying to sustain their long-distant 'relationship'. Everyone had heard stories of guys doing goofy things under similar circumstances. As his friend, I wanted him to stop obsessing. Perhaps I could get him to think about something else?

Tony casually mentioned that his father worked for the government and he had spent some time living in Turkey. As a guy from Roseville Michigan, I was fascinated about what it must have been like to live in such an exotic place. Tony answered my endless questions about faraway Turkey. One of his stories was about some Turkish guy who had taught him how to throw a knife. I happened to own a knife,

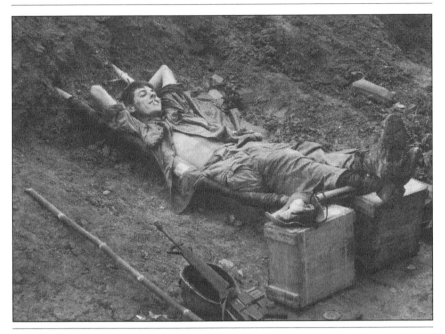

Photo by Tony Hallas

wanted to see if he could demonstrate his skill and maybe show me how to throw my knife.

One night, when I was still with Bandido Charlie, I happened to be lying on a rice paddy dike and got the idea that I needed a weapon that could be used in close quarters. What if someone crept silently, in the dark, through the rice? They would be right on top of us in no time at all. Would I be able to swing my machine gun around quickly enough to shoot? A machine gun would make a lousy club. The next time I saw a roadside vendor, with the right kind of knife, I bought it.

As luck would have it, I chose the exact same kind of knife that the Viet Cong carried. It was a largish Bowie-style black blade with a black wooden handle. The blade was untempered black steel. This was NOT a pretty, gleaming, sculptured steel blade kind-of-knife.

This was a mean-looking knife, sheathed in a black leather scabbard. Some people might compare the sharpness of a knife blade to something known for sharpness like a razor. My knife's blade had a sharpness that was less sophisticated. It was sharp the same way a broken beer bottle is sharp. I wore it everyday, even after I had transferred to the PIO. Jungle fatigue shirts have big pockets and are worn over the belt, not tucked in like all other military shirts. Even though it was rather large, my unauthorized weapon was concealed, most of the time. It hung on my belt, covered by my fatigue shirt, out-of-sight. Any Vietnamese, who might have caught a glimpse of it, assumed that I had taken my knife from a Viet Cong. I said nothing to discourage the illusion. A girl once asked me about the VC I had to have killed in order to take his knife. Tony said that my knife was a little oversized and heavy for throwing, but had the right kind of balance.

Tony tossed my knife and almost casually buried the blade in the darkroom wall. He was clearly proficient at knife throwing. Tony patiently explained that speed, spin and arc were the variables that needed to be controlled for properly sticking a knife into someone. We took my knife outside, for my education in the finer points of knife hurling. Hours were spent perfecting my knife throwing skills. It took several days before I could be somewhere close being as good as Tony was at sticking my knife into the trees outside the lab. An electric grinder, at the motor pool, was used to put a sharp edge back onto my flat black blade.

Tony was an excellent photographer, handy with a knife and was also a virtuoso guitar player. Tony Hallas played Flamenco and Classic Spanish guitar. Hallas bought a smallish looking acoustic guitar from the gift shop next-door. At first, he just chucked it up onto storage space over the photo lab's interior door/light-trap ceiling. Tony claimed that he couldn't play the guitar because it had metal strings. Tony elucidated about how metal strings would cut-up his fingers. He had written his psycho girlfriend and asked her to send him some gut strings. Tony waited until they arrived before he would even attempt to play his new guitar. It was worth the wait.

I appreciate a wide variety of music. I started playing concert string bass in junior high and continued to play in the Roseville High School Concert Band. My high school band played mostly classical music. As an extra circular entrepreneurial activity, I used my public school's bass to play in a variety of pick-up bands. These improvised pick-up ensembles played standards, some swing, jazz, even polkas, and a very little country. I did not play rock n' roll. For me holding a bass guitar felt awkward and using frets was confusing. As a kid, I listened to my father's big bands records. My mother liked swing and eventually rock.

When I was ten years old, my mother brought home a 45 recording of Elvis Presley singing *Heartbreak Hotel*. Mom and I played that record until it became nearly transparent.

So, I had been a fan since rock started to roll. I firmly believed that Jimmy Hendrix was easily the best guitarist that ever played. Then I heard Tony Hallas play.

After his gut strings arrived, Hallas started to hone his guitar playing skills and, in Tony's case, those skills were considerable. Hallas' new six-string acoustic guitar was slightly larger than a four-string ukulele.

Tony didn't read, or need, sheet music. He intuitively, seemingly effortlessly, made his new guitar sing. Hallas' technique was tight and precise. Tony played guitar with feeling and passion. I had never heard such beautifully intricate melodies. The darkroom resonated with complex classical guitar compositions. His music was alive with intricate riffs that spiraled into complex harmonies. Playing guitar with both hands independently Tony could simultaneously pluck and strum his strings.

It was fascinating to watch Hallas perform. His movements were smooth and sometimes surprising, like when he would unexpectedly begin beating out a rhythm on his guitar's body, right in the middle of an intricate improvisational riff. Every song was memorable. Watching and listening to Tony Hallas play Classical Spanish Guitar definitely expanded my musical horizons. Jimmy Hendrix would no longer top my list of guitar heroes.

JAY SMITH'S LEGACY

Jay Smith left a generous legacy behind when he returned to the United States. He gave all of us the cantankerous, always entertaining and sometimes affectionate Charlie Gibbon. Jay personally provided me with an excellent part-time job at the Officer's Club. But his most generous bequest was the Public Information Office Photo Lab. It was a private office, air conditioned sanctuary, and a great place to just hang-out.

Tony Hallas and I did some outstanding photographic work in that darkroom.

Rest and Relaxation destinations, as well as the Cho Lon PX in Saigon, offered hugely discounted prices on photo and electronic equipment. My fellow correspondents were welcome to store their recently acquired, state-of-the-art, stereo equipment in the relatively clean, secure and temperature-controlled confines of the PIO darkroom. Many of our contemporaries accepted our offer to secure their stuff. The broadcast specialists were especially astute about the features of the latest stereo equipment and even used the darkroom to test-out their new stuff.

The laboratory walls were plastered with anti-war posters that were only visible when the white lights were on. The overall effect of air conditioning, controlled lighting, bitchin' music and anti-war wall décor made the darkroom a cool, almost civilian, island in a military sea. The place literally rocked.

All lights had to be off when film was being processed. Absolute darkness was essential. The room lights still had to be off when prints were being made. However, one muted yellow safe light could be used to illuminate the otherwise light sensitive photographic paper when prints were being made. I was working at this very process one day when the outside door opened. Light from the office instantly filled the light trap and leaked through the seams in its loose construction. Even more light came through the gaps in the curtains that had been hung to compensate for the light trap's shortcomings. The photograph I was making was about to be ruined.

"In or out! But shut that God damned door!" I shouted. "You're letting all the darkness out."

The door closed. Someone bumped into the wall that formed the first right-angle turn in the lab's light-trap maze. I held back a chuckle. The in-coming visitors almost fell again when they got tangled in the curtains at the end of the light-trap. Finally two figures, wearing steel combat helmets, stumbled their way to the table where I was working. Shallow trays of chemical solution lay on the table under a low-hung amber 'safe light' fixture. The dim 'safe light' was the lab's only illumination. The anti-war posters covering the walls were concealed in darkness. Together, my visitors and I watched an image slowly materialize on the light-sensitive paper floating in the chemical solution.

"I have to continuously agitate the solution. The movement keeps a fresh supply of chemistry in contact with the paper's surface and promotes faster and more even development." I explained to the mute spectators. They hadn't introduced themselves and just grunted their understanding. Eventually, I transferred the print, momentarily, to another tray with acid stop bath. Finally the print went into a third tray containing chemical fixer for an extended soak.

One of them asked, "Can we turn the lights on now?"

"NO." I exclaimed. "We have to wait for the fixative to do its work. It takes a while for the sodium thiosulfate to neutralize the white light sensitive properties in the chemicals that coat the paper. We can't turn on the lights until that happens. If we turn the lights on now, the white light would turn the paper black. Even after the chemistry does its work, we'll still have to wash all that stuff off the print in clear water. A print has to be washed for a half hour or so before it can be dried. We're at least 45 minutes away from being able to show anyone a regular photograph."

"I see," said one of the men as they turned to leave. "Well, carry on and thanks for the demonstration."

They probably wouldn't have appreciated the poster.

Later, I discovered that the Division's Commanding General and the Adjutant General had paid me a visit. If I had recognized them, or if they had introduced themselves, I would have followed protocol, stood at attention, and saluted or something. As it was, I was glad that I didn't have the white lights on.

SERGEANT FIRST CLASS STEVENSON

My friend Tony was indirectly responsible for Sergeant First Class Stevenson wanting to have me court-martialed.

When Tony and I transferred into the PIO, the office was located in a tent close to the other Division Headquarters sections. It was part of an administrative complex one block away from the sheet metal building that contained the darkroom/photo lab. Tony and I spent most of our time out searching for stories or working at our air-conditioned Photo Lab. No one gave much thought about the photographers never being around the office. Sergeant First Class Stevenson had called a first-thing-in-the morning correspondents meeting at the regular PIO tent/office. I was at the meeting, Tony Hallas was not.

Sergeant First Class Stevenson, " Sondy, where's Hallas?"

"Hell, if I know Sarge, it wasn't my day to watch him."

Everyone at the meeting snickered, everyone except Sergeant First Class Stevenson. He did not think that my smart-ass retort was funny. He instantly forgot about Tony Hallas. I had made him lose face, in front of all the correspondents. I was now, and forever, on the top of his shit list.

Aside from that one little slip, I had an enormous amount of respect for that particular Army Lifer. Sergeant First Class Stevenson really was an outstanding non-commissioned officer. Unlike a lot of other Sergeants, Sergeant First Class Stevenson seriously considered the best interests of those who worked under him. He had given me good council on multiple occasions. Sergeant First Class Stevenson had a Morgan Freeman kind of gravitas and paternal warmth. I liked Sergeant First Class Stevenson.

For the record: I was instantly sorry for having made that flippant remark to the good Sergeant. I regretted it the moment those words had escaped my lips. However, I could not apologize my way out of this dumb mistake. I could not apologize because an expression of regret would have broken one of those 'unwritten' Army rules: *Never tell a Sergeant that you are "sorry."*

In the Army the word *sorry* is a *trigger.* An automatic conditioned response is hard-wired into all non-commissioned officers and violating this implicit statute by using the word *sorry* will invariably set it off. Any Sergeant hearing that word will

My WWII M2 carbine with selector switch.

be compelled to elaborate on just how *sorry* you are. These denunciations always evolve into extended rants. These tirades are required to include references gender, sexual preference, and genetic heritage and are prone to continue for several minutes. A lecturing Sergeant's volume must be maximized in order to dramatize the subject's humiliation and insure the public

1st Infantry Division Public Information Office Staff, 1968

mortification of anyone thoughtless enough to say the word *sorry*. So I never apologized. Stevenson never got to vent and I wound-up on every shit detail that Sergeant First Class Stevenson could think of. Not satisfied, Sergeant First Class Stevenson would even attempt to have me court-marital. Apparently, I really pissed him off.

The morning I reported for KP, the company cook thought that I was joking. No one drew KP. Cooks headed the kitchen, Vietnamese did the work. Together, they kept the mess hall spotless, prepared the food and served the GI's. They formed a team and didn't need my help. After dishing-out dehydrated scrambled eggs, the cook sent me away until it was time to serve lunch. After lunch the cook said that I didn't have to come back to serve dinner and, if I ever drew KP again, I could take the day off because he would cover for me. The only time the cooks wanted to see me in the mess hall was when I was eating. I didn't have to come back to work KP.

Guard duty was another matter. When I first transferred into the First Administration Company I had somehow managed to be "overlooked" when it came to guard duty. Those days were gone. Now, I was scheduled to stand guard every couple of weeks. It was kind of a nuisance. But it was nothing compared to being in the field.

The NCO in charge of the Officer's Club -(where I operated the movie projector) would provide an excuse to get out of guard duty whenever I asked. He would claim that the officers needed to see a movie. When I actually did stand guard, I was one of the few men who had actually fired a weapon after basic training.

When I was with the 1st BN 16th INF every moment–24/7–was some degree of *guard duty*. There was always a loaded weapon in easy reach. As a REMF, I was assigned a camera. But, weapons were only available to members of the 1st Admin Company on those irregular occasions when we pulled a more formal, almost stateside, version of guard duty. There was a company armory and we would draw M-16s. However, not having a weapon close at hand in a battlefield situation promotes a certain feeling of insecurity.

Therefore, I bought a WWII M-2 carbine with a selector switch, the switch made my carbine fully automatic. My folding stock carbine (paratrooper model) was a machine pistol that fit perfectly into the left outside leg pocket of my fatigue pants— I'm a southpaw. Two thirty-round magazines fit into the pocket on my right thigh. A 500-round box of ammunition, included in the purchase price, was stashed in my locker. I only carried the carbine when I was covering a story *out in the field*.

Sergeant First Class Stevenson's nefarious scheme to reprimand, and eventually court-marital, me was tied into a CQ (Charge of Quarters) duty assignment. Charge of Quarters required sitting at Sgt. Stevenson's desk, after normal hours of operation, all night, to answer the phone. Sitting there was as boring as it was pointless. Since the reason for being there was more punitive than practical, no specific instructions were given about what to do if the phone did actually ring. I was told to simply sit there and wait for the phone to ring. It rang exactly once.

The unexpected call was startling. This was a 'field' phone, the receiver sat in a box. The box had a cover that closed to protect the phone when it was used outside (in the field). There was a crank on the side for outgoing calls. Outgoing calls were made by turning the crank and asking a switchboard operator to be connected to another phone. For incoming calls the phone simply rang, like any other phone. I answered the phone with a cheerful, "First Infantry

Division PIO". My greeting was the only pleasant part of that entire phone answering experience.

The only difference between Public Information Office and Public Information Officer is the letter **R**. The person and the institution share the same acronym: PIO. The bonehead on the other end of the phone couldn't, *or wouldn't,* understand that he had reached the OFFICE and not the PERSON. I repeatedly explained to the caller that I was not the Public Information Officer. Several times I clearly stated that the caller had, in fact, reached the Public Information Office. Our conversation lasted for several minutes. To an eavesdropper, our dialogue would have sounded like the Abbot and Costello sketch about *Who's On First.*

At one point, I even offered to have someone find the Public Information Officer and bring him to the phone, all the while not having any idea how I could make that happen.

I asked for contact information so the PIO could return the call. The caller refused to co-operate. Finally, the inquiring genius gave-up and hung-up.

The next day Sergeant First Class Stevenson told me that he had filed an official reprimand. He flatly stated that I was guilty of *impersonating an officer* and that I would receive, at the very least, an Article 15—I might even be court-martialed.

Sergeant First Class Stevenson never bothered to ask me any questions.

Major Chick had been promoted from his position as the First Infantry Division Public Information Officer to another position at the Military Assistance Command Vietnam, in Saigon. The new Public Information Officer was Major Vitello. Vitello, the new Public Information Officer, would eventually be promoted to Lieutenant Colonel. Vitello did ask me about what had transpired. I explained, leaving out the paranoid part about Sergeant First Class Stevenson wanting revenge for my indiscrete remark. Major Vitello understood what an acronym was. Just when it appeared that there would be some kind of *final showdown,* someone in Sergeant First Class Stevenson's family died. He went home on a thirty-day compassionate leave. The matter was dropped.

When he returned I had been promoted to Specialist 4th Class.

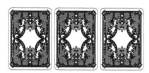

JOSEPH B. LOVELL

The lesson involving acceptable use of acronyms while on the phone also provided a valuable lesson about the mechanics of utilizing the office's field phone. I put my new-found knowledge to use the second time I was assigned Charge of Quarters (CQ) duty. I was inspired by boredom and was presented with the opportunity to call my old friend Joe Lovell. Joe played saxophone in the Roseville High School Concert Band, graduated one year before me, was one of my best friends, and happened to be repairing jet engines at an Air Force Base just south of Cam Rhan Bay.

Joseph Burt Lovell had joined the Air Force shortly after high school to avoid becoming a pedestrian. Joe had chosen not to attend college. Electing to not extend his education had eliminated any chance for qualifying for student deferment while, at the same time, presented Lovell with the opportunity to develop a hobby. Joe had taken-up the sport of street drag racing to fill-in his spare time. Joe's sporting interest also provided him with the opportunity to pile-up some major points on his driving record. Lovell had accumulated twice as many points as the State of Michigan allowed for possessing a valid motor vehicle license. Joe was certain to have his driver's license revoked while simultaneously not addressing the *draft* problem that plagued every other healthy young American male citizen. These circumstances combined to ignite Joe's heretofore-repressed patriotism. Lovell reasoned that the Air Force was a better place, than the Army, for satisfying his patriotic fervor. Joe's military career path began with a potential arrest warrant in Michigan and ended with his repairing jet engines at Phan Rang Air Base in Vietnam.

Danger Main was the First Infantry Division telephone exchange. I simply turned the field phone's crank and asked the *Danger Main* operator to patch a call through to Phan Rang Air Force Base. The

Public Information Office had a black and white TV. Two broadcast stations offered viewers limited choices: One station broadcast exclusively in Vietnamese and the other was Armed Forces Vietnam. AFVN stopped broadcasting at 2330 Hours. The last show, before their sign-off was *Bobbie the Weather Girl*. I watched Bobbie while I waited for my call to go through the various military phone networks. The weather girl was a leggy blond. She always wore short mini-dresses, displaying shapely legs. Bobbie always gave one of two predictable forecasts: hot & wet or hot & dry. Bobbie bounced around doing an awkward sort of pantomimed dance at the end of her show. The camera would pan-in to a close-up of her very attractive face as she teased her audience with the flirty *double entendre*, "Have a nice day weather-wise and otherwise."

With the help of at least a half a dozen intermediate switchboard operators, I was finally able to speak with the CQ at Joe's squadron. It took another twenty minutes for a runner to track-down Lovell at his barracks, and drag him to the phone. We had kept in touch through the mail. My late-night phone call was a total surprise.

I hadn't seen Joe for over a year. Lovell said that I was lucky to have caught-up with him. He had just come back from a weekend pass in Saigon. I told him about how complicated it was to make an inter-service in-country phone call. We talked quickly and caught-up on some of the recent stuff we had done. I asked Joe how we might be able to meet-up in Saigon. Joe's job limited his getting away and he didn't have as much access to transportation as I did. Meeting in Saigon could be problematic.

It seemed as if seeing my old friend wasn't going to happen. I asked Joe for more details about the logistics for his recent trip to Saigon from Phan Rang. He said that he had gone north to Cam Ranh Bay before heading south to Tan Son Nhut. Cam Ranh Bay and Phan Rang were both considerably outside my normal area of operation. But, I had had used my press pass to go all the way to Hawaii, at least a trip to Phan Rang would be inside the same country. Depending on what kind of aircraft I could snag a ride on, backtracking Joe's route should be a piece of cake.

I could probably find my way to Phan Rang in a couple of hours. Sometimes Joe had to work weekends. He had time off on the weekend coming up. But, he probably couldn't get permission to go

to Saigon two weekends in a row. Our call ended with me saying that I would see him sometime Friday. Although, I wasn't sure about exactly when I would arrive. I knew that flights left Bien Hoa and Tan Son Nhut at all hours because night time flight schedules were preferable for supply flight crews. Planes were less likely to be shot while under the cover of darkness.

I left Lai Khe just before dinner and landed in Phan Rang at dusk. Lai Khe to Bien Hoa and Tan Son Nhut were little helicopter hops. Saigon to Cam Ranh and Phan Rang required persuading a couple of different Air Force enlisted men that I was indeed entitled to priority one travel.

In Phan Rang, there were regular shuttle buses going to the various squadron areas. I caught a bus that would take me to Joe's barracks. It traveled west through the northern portion of a very large base. On the left, there were major runways with F4 Phantoms and A10 Growlers taking off at regular intervals. A compound identified by South Korean signage was visible through the windows on the right side there, was. It was meticulously organized, spotlessly clean and brightly lit. Dusk was changing into dark. Korean troops, wearing white t-shirts were running around in formation and doing physical training drills in the cooling breezes. Beyond all that, Joe's barracks was one of a cluster of cinderblock buildings set back from the west side of the runway complex. I asked directions to the Squadron's Orderly Room. Joe had told them I was coming and an airman walked me over to his building.

Air Force barracks were long two-story shoebox shaped buildings just like stateside Army barracks, except they were built with cinderblocks instead of being made from wood framing and clapboard siding. I guessed that the block construction would provide better sound insulation against all those noisy jets taking-off and landing. The interior of barracks was divided into two-man cubicles, like the nicest NCO barracks back at Ft. Benning. These barracks had one additional feature that made them better than any Army barracks— *totally silent central air conditioning*. When I was a Grunt I slept fully clothed, usually on the ground, exposed to the weather and wildlife. As a REMF I felt privileged to have a cot, inside a tent, with a mosquito net and a poncho liner for covers.

The Air Force had one more surprising element in their accommodations: *modern plumbing*. Even Air Force enlisted men had flush toilets and variable temperature showers. Air Force latrines weren't communal like the Army. Airmen had individual stalls! Army showers, officers and enlisted men alike, were a shared arrangement. Fifty-five-gallon drums of water were suspended overhead, on a wooden framework, and air temperature water delivered by a gravity-flow system. Rope-pull valves connected to minimalist spigots, regulated the water. Even the staff-grade officers in Lai Khe, used outhouses that relied on shit-burning technology. I could see why guys enlisted in the Air Force.

Joe hadn't changed much since I had last seen him. He was still skinny, had thinning blond hair and still smoked Tareytons. Joe asked if I was hungry. I told him that I had skipped dinner. So, we went to the mess hall. The Air Force worked three shifts. So food was available almost anytime. We did some more catching-up over dinner. No one seemed to notice that I was the only Army person in the room.

"So what's with all those Korean guys I passed on the way here?" I asked.

"This place is guarded by the U.S. Army, Australians and the South Koreans," he said.

"So, do you get attacked very often?" I inquired between mouthfuls of mess hall fare.

Joe said, "Naw, once in a while they might shoot some rockets at us. We all go hide in the bunker. But they usually don't hit anything. The worst thing might be a hole blown into the runway. Take-offs and landings might shut-down for a half hour, tops. There just aren't many VC around here. The Koreans scared them away."

"How'd they do that?" I asked.

"The Koreans are crazy." Joe stated matter-of-factly.

"I saw their compound on the way here." I said. "They looked strange, running around and doing PT. It looked like they've got more painted rocks than the Army. And where did they get all those sandbags? That place looks like some kind of castle. Anybody who does that kind of work, in this heat, has to be nuts."

"No, its way worse than that." Joe said. "When they catch someone that they even think is an enemy sympathizer, they torture him, in public, in front of everybody. When they're done they just execute the poor son-of-a-bitch, right there on the spot. It's like entertainment for them. Those guys are CRAZY. And, before you ask, no I couldn't watch something like that."

Seeing a need to change the subject, "You said that there's Australians here. What are they like? Are they crazy too?"

"The Aussies are OK." Lovell said. "They're a little *unusual*. But they're definitely not crazy like the Koreans."

"How 'strange' can they be?" I asked.

"The Aussies have this weird thing about being a 'man'." He said. "I guess that it's more like the way that they have to prove their manhood all the time. It's an obsession. What's really strange is their thing about being 'macho' doesn't involve women. They're more concerned about proving their manliness to one another. Aussies don't mess with the women like normal guys. They just hang-out together and play strange drinking games."

"Come on, how weird can a drinking game be?"

Joe said, "OK, you asked for it. Take this game for example:

Two guys will stand eye-to-eye close. Both of them will have a glass of beer in their hand. Each guy, with his free hand (the one that ain't holding the beer), reaches into the other guy's pants. They grab a patch of the other guy's pubic hair as they stare, intently grim-faced, into each other's eyes. A third guy will count down and, on the count of three, both guys yank out the hair that they they're holding. The guy who flinches is the loser."

"Sounds painful. What could anyone win that would be worth playing such an awful game? Do they play for money?" I asked.

"No." Lovell said. He had a sadistic grin spreading over his face. "They put all the freshly extracted hair into the loser's beer. The loser has to chug the beer, hairs and all. Maybe you'll see them do it tomorrow. I am planning to take you to the Strip."

"Cool. Is the Strip in downtown Phan Rang?" I asked.

"No, the strip is really in the middle of nowhere, just south of the base. It's really kind of neat." Joe said.

He continued, "The base commander got tired of the guys going into town and tearing-up the place. So, he made the city of Phan Rang off-limits and had a place special-built for the men's entertainment. The Strip looks like a movie set from a cowboy movie. It has one dusty street, two blocks long. Wooden "boardwalk-style" sidewalks line the street. Even though it looks like a cowboy western town, there are no horses or hitching posts. In fact, there's never any traffic on the street. All of the businesses are the same: all bars. But they are not all alike. Each bar has a theme and caters to a different audience. There are a couple of places the black guys like and some that are targeted for the Australians. The prices are fixed. A beer will cost no more than a dollar and a hooker is $5.00. Patrons sit down stairs drinking beer while they decided which girl they want to spend short-time with. If a girl looks interesting, you buy her a Saigon Tea. Saigon Tea is just a $5 shot-glass filled with Kool Aid. It's a way for the 'house' to turn a profit. The girl will sit and flirt as long as you keep buying Saigon Teas. The 'house' keeps all the money from Saigon Tea sales. If you want to take your companion up stairs for a 'short time' the 'house' will get half of her $5 fee. She gets to keep any additional tip. So, if you ever plan on seeing her again it's a good idea to give her a tip. It's probably a good idea to leave a tip anyway.

"There are also two 'Tea Houses.' We'll go there first. The girls working in the 'Tea Houses' are special. Besides wearing Japanese kimonos and serving regular real tea (the Tea Houses don't sell alcohol) the Tea House girls aren't available for 'short time'. They just flirt. But they're better looking than the hookers. I think the Tea Houses are more for the married guys or those up-tight religious types. But still, its kind of fun in a strange straight-laced sort of way."

"This Strip sounds like a sexual Disneyland." I said. "Aren't you worried about catching something? I've heard that they won't let you go home if you've got the clap."

"No problem. The CO has got that covered, too." Joe said. "Once a month the medics go through the whole place and shoot everything that breaths full of Penicillin. I've heard they even go after stray dogs. No one has ever caught anything and we have the healthiest hookers in Asia."

"That would make a hell of a welcome sign." I said.

"Population: 0"
Joe corrected me.
"No one actually
lives there. Its only
open noon till dark.
Everybody that works
there commutes."

The next day we
spent the morning
touring the base. Joe
took me around to the hangar where he worked, the Base Exchange and other places he thought I would find interesting. After lunch we caught a ride on another shuttle. It was really a steak truck without seats. We stood with about a dozen other guys, for the ten-minute trip.

The Strip was exactly like Joe had described it. However, precise memories of The Strip are sort of vague. I may have set a record for the number of Bam Nee Bas consumed. Since refrigeration is a costly luxury, all beer was served in glasses over ice. Schlitz was the popular American brand. Bam Nee Ba was the Vietnamese interpretation of beer. Ice diluted and disguised Bam Nee Ba's distinctive flavor. Melting ice also cloaked the local beer's accelerated alcohol content. Bam Nee Ba translates to the number thirty-three, those numbers were the only recognizable symbols on the well-worn bottles' French label. No Korean troops went to The Strip. There were Australians. They did get drunk and rowdy. The Aussies may have even played the drinking game Joe described. I can't remember much about specific occurrences.

After that initial trip, I visited Phan Rang a total of three more times. On my final, visit, I found that the Air Base's new commander had bulldozed The Strip. The city of Phan Rang was still off-limits. Although it was hard to tell the city was verboten, with the high number of uniformed personnel walking around on its streets. Most of the activity that used to happen on The Strip had moved east of Phan Rang to the beach. The beach was not off-limits. The city of Phan Rang is located on the coast of the South China Sea. The heavily guarded beach was surrounded by sand dunes and populated with beer, food and sex vendors. Working girls plied their trade in the shallow surf. Even though the buildings with the cowboy town motif were gone, the party had simply moved. The old western theme had been replaced with the Beach Boys' sun, surf and sand.

BOB MANCINI

Personnel in Vietnam were always changing. One-year tours of duty meant that everyone was replaced *eventually*. Back in Lai Khe, a freshly minted 2nd Lieutenant replaced the old NCO who had previously managed the Officer's Club. The change in management didn't effect my part-time job as the club's twice-a-week movie projectionist. My seniority and private projectionist ability has secured my access to unlimited free beer. The club's new manager asked if I wanted to expand my function and become a bartender. Accepting the barkeep job would have meant giving-up my regular job at the PIO. I did not want that to happen.

I recommended someone else: BOB MANCINI.

Bob, like Tony Hallas and myself, was another grunt rescued by Major Chick. When I first met Bob he had been a stringer out in some field unit. Mancini sent in badly exposed film along with his stories. Bob was <u>not</u> a great photographer. He was a decent writer. Bob and Vince Spadafora (still another salvaged infantryman) played poker in an impromptu poker tournament that I sometimes participated in. Our poker games convened, at irregular intervals, in a variety of undisclosed locations. Bob took the job as a bartender.

Before Bob stared working at the Officers' Club I would receive free drinks, along with two dollars for showing movies. My job-referral had extended my free drinking privilege. Bob expanded my access to the bar to anytime he was working. My bar tab was *unlimited* when ever Bob was behind the bar.

Among many other responsibilities, Lieutenant Brandt was the Public Information Office's Acquisition Officer. He had procured my new camera. Brandt was also the manager for KLIK, the First Infantry Division's rock n' roll radio station. One day, Lieutenant Brandt came to me with a warning. Someone was advancing a

Tony Hallas, Bob Mancini and Dominic Sondy (left-right)

petition at the Officer's Club accusing me of allegedly abusing my drinking privileges. According to Lieutenant Brandt, some Captain from the Military Intelligence Section, had authored a petition to have me banned from the club. I was shocked that an officer would pick-on a humble Specialist 4th Class for drinking an occasional beer. I felt compelled to investigate this miscarriage of authority.

I took my usual stool at the bar sitting next to a Warrant Officer. Warrant Officers were mostly helicopter pilots. Their ranking status was somewhere between non-commissioned officers (Sergeants) and regular commissioned officers (Lieutenants and above). Regular officers looked down on WOs while non-coms ignored them. I liked Warrant Officers. Helicopter pilots had one of the riskiest jobs in the Army, they never seemed to get enough credit, especially the medivac pilots. I bought the guy a beer and, with a wink, told Mancini to put it on my tab.

I leaned over the bar and, in a conspiratorial whisper, asked, "Bob, have you heard anything about some weird petition about me?"

Mancini broke into a broad grin and said, "Sure, I have it right here." He reached under the counter and laid a document down in front of me. "Some moron gave me this and told me to have people sign it. No one has asked me about it and I sure as hell am not going to solicit signatures." The petition sported two signatures. "I was going to ask you what you wanted me to do with it. Should I just throw it away?"

"I don't know." I said. "If the petition disappears, the guy might try to start another one. If you hang-on to it, and nobody signs it, he would probably have to give up."

Bob said, "What do you think would happen if we embarrassed the guy? Say we put a bunch of bogus signatures on his petition, like Mickey Mouse and Goofy. If he ever showed it to anyone they would just laugh at him." Then Mancini declared, "This is a bar. At least Jim Beam and Johnny Walker should sign it." He scribbled one name, switched hands, and scrawled another.

The petition, with double the number of signatures, was returned to its obscure position on the shelf under the bar. The petition was still on that shelf, under the bar, when I left Vietnam.

KEVIN KELLY

The First Infantry Division Public Information Office had at least two-dozen men on its full-time staff. There were writers, photographers, a half-dozen officers, clerks, a combat artist, a fair number of broadcast specialists and one dispatch driver. One of the broadcast specialists' official mission was to record "Hometown Interviews". These were taped dialogue with GIs that were designated for distribution to local radio stations back in the States. Hometown interviews were oral 'letters from the front,' a kind of cross between an audio newsreel and public letter to everyone in a GI's hometown. However, the broadcast specialists at the PIO were mostly interested in playing rock n roll on *KLIK*.

KLIK was a 24-hour, rock n' roll *pirate* radio station. It had a format that sounded as fresh, professional and as up-to-date as any of the new FM stations back home; there was one notable exception: there were very few commercials. The KLIK play-list was totally unrestricted and disc jockeys played current music, news and sports. KLIK was the sound of home for GIs within its considerable broadcast range. It was like a beacon broadcasting Americana into the heat, humidity and rot of war-torn Vietnam. KLIK was a morale booster for its listeners and a source of pride for the men who contributed to its programming. A freshly-minted celebrity disc jockey replacement was expected. Understandably, the jocks were excited about the arrival of a famous west coast radio star. He was supposed to enhance to *KLIK*'s reputation for genuine 'stateside' quality entertainment.

Kevin Kelly was assigned to the PIO after working as a genuine full-time on-air radio personality in California. He was alleged to be personally familiar with a wide range of West Coast groups from *The Beach Boys* to *The Doors*. Kevin Kelly was cool, charismatic and possibly one exception to the *Treat Replacements Like Shit* rule. Kevin was a genuinely likable person. Initially, Kelly was welcomed onto the PIO team.

Kevin had *national* reputation. Just about everyone, except those of us from the East and the Midwest, had heard his radio show. I was one of the few people who hadn't heard him and avoided pandering his celebrity. I was surprised when Kevin sought me out. I was alone, reading a book in the cool air-conditioned comfort of my darkroom, when he stopped to visit. After some almost awkward small talk, Kevin revealed the ulterior motive for his visit.

"You seem like the kinda guy who knows his way around." Kevin said as he meandered toward his point, "*Do you know where I could find some pot?*" was the reason for his unexpected visit.

The thought of some kind of Sergeant First Class Stevenson set-up seemed paranoid. I dismissed this fleeting thought and I considered Kevin's request. I had never smoked pot and knew that the Army frowned on people with a taste for the unorthodox. Still, this guy was a notable personality and scrounging-up something for Kevin Kelly presented a challenge that might represent rewards down the road.

Vietnam had a reputation for drugs. But, I had absolutely no experience in this area. My innocents was more of a practical choice than a moral judgment. Back at Bandido Charlie, my friends didn't smoke pot or do anything drug related–*except alcohol*.

The reality being that it had been hard enough to stay alert while being physically exhausted and sleep deprived. Being stoned would only have made it too easy to become dead. No one wanted to die, or be the irresponsible reason for someone else's death. So, we simply didn't do drugs.

True, not all units were like Bandido Charlie. And, I knew that REMFs were another matter; they didn't face the same level of risk and could probably afford to take a recreational chance. I try to avoid making judgments about other people's behavior and simply hadn't considered buying pot until Kevin asked me. His request was a challenge to my logistical skill.

"Well, Kevin I don't know." Disappointment flashed across his face. "I haven't ever scored any pot before. But, I think that I know where I could find some for you. Give me a couple of days and I'll see what I can do."

My intuition told me to begin my search locally. The next day I hitched a ride with a convoy and hopped off at the first firebase we came to. I went directly the open-air bazaar that was located just outside the firebase's gate. Almost every roadside firebase had a temporary daytime market located near its gate. The empty stretches of road could be dangerous. Firebases offered vendors some security. By late afternoon the tents would be gone and the entrepreneurs would have left. Before leaving they would have done a brisk business selling beer, soda, cigarettes, jewelry, food, sex and drugs. The highway's constant traffic, and the GIs, provided a constant stream of customers.

I asked one of the merchants to help me find the momma-san who might be selling pot, found her, and bought some pot for Kevin. I took some "stock" pictures, to provide an excuse for my trip, and headed back to Lai Khe. I was lucky enough to catch a helicopter that had just finished delivering some replacements. Having returned in time for dinner, I caught up with Kelly at the mess hall and suggested that he meet me at the photo lab.

Kevin knocked and walked into the lab. I tossed him a package, wrapped in Vietnamese newspaper and told him that he owed me five dollars in Vietnamese money.

That was equivalent to about $3.00 in Military Payment Certificates. MPC, passed for money in an economy that was supposed to be void of greenback dollars. Kevin's eyes lit-up when he unrolled the paper. He was holding over an ounce of what I later found was primo weed. I asked him not to fire one up inside my darkroom. Kevin was astounded at the price. He couldn't believe how inexpensive it was and insisted on giving a 35mm film can full of pot, as a "commission," for making the deal. I didn't know what to do with my unexpected "windfall." I hadn't smoked pot, didn't especially want or have a need for it. There wasn't enough of it, in that little container, to sell and I couldn't think of anyone, in the Army, to give it to. So, I stashed it in the lab until I could mail it to a friend back home.

Less than a week later, Kevin asked me if I could find some more pot for him. What was he doing with this stuff? I incorrectly guessed that it must take a lot of pot to do whatever pot did. Buying pot, the first time, had not been difficult or inconvenient. So, I did it again. Kevin gave me another film container full of pot. He insisted that I take it. I didn't want a "commission"; I had done it as a favor.

I went back to my hooch one afternoon to discover how wrong I had been about needing a lot of pot to do whatever pot did. One of the five guys living my hooch (tent) happened to come home while I was in the process of learning about the error of assumption about Vietnamese pot's potency. I wound up giving the second film can of pot to my hooch mate.

Kevin asked me to buy him some more pot a third time. I declined. However, I suggested that he could come "out into the field" with me. Then, he could buy his own pot and eliminate me from the now awkward position of being his supplier.

We set out on our expedition the next day. The first step was to let the office know that we were leaving. It was routine, and expected, for everyone to go "out in the field" to cover assignments. Nonetheless, we always had to sign-out. A photographer and broadcast specialist two-man team was irregular. Usually I would operate alone or, sometimes, work with a writer. The *Hometown Interviews* that Kevin would be collecting were designated for radio stations back home. My pictures weren't going to be part of the Kevin's work package. But having Kevin travel with someone with experience was something our supervisors thought of as a good idea. Kelly was new and his leaving with me was seen as a show of initiative and demonstrated his enthusiasm for the new PIO team member's mission. Our cleverness earned 'brownie points' for both of us.

I showed Kevin where the airstrip was and the procedure for catching a helicopter ride. We checked in at the tent that served as the airstrip's control center.

Our press credentials would have taken us anywhere. We were careful to find a helicopter that was supplying a firebase that wasn't (under attack) hot and made sure that there would be another flight scheduled to bring us back today. I was showing Kevin the ropes; not trying scare the shit out of him. Besides, having Kevin spend the night in a place where he might be shot at would have been counter productive to my objective; which was to make it so easy for Kevin. I wanted him to go out and buy his own pot.

As we walked in the direction of the chopper that would take us out of Lai Khe Kevin asked, "How do you know that the person who sells you pot will be at this particular firebase?"

"That's easy, I don't know exactly know who will be selling us pot. I don't have a special 'contact'." I said, "Some firebases are located near roads. Roads have people on them. Many of those people are willing to sell you stuff. The selling people show-up in the morning and leave in time to be home before curfew. You'll see. These folks sell all kinds of stuff. You could probably buy the same things in Saigon. But roadside people sell everything cheaper.

"The problem is that roadside vendors aren't completely reputable. They travel like gypsies. They spend one day at one base, then go to another base another day. The same vendor will move around to several firebases. They'll rip you off in a minute because the odds are pretty good that you will never see them again. So, you have to be careful.

"There are probably a couple of more things you should know: Never buy a watch from anyone except the PX. Roadside vendors sell watches that look just like the real expensive ones. But they're all crap. One time I bought a watch that looked just like a Seiko. It looked exactly like the kind they sell in the PX. This was a diver's model with a rotating bevel, a black face, glow-in-the-dark numbers, and, of course, it was supposed to be waterproof. All that, and the seller was only asking five bucks for it! The day after I bought it the crystal clouded-up with moisture. Then, the moisture turned pink with rust. It quit working in less than a week. The bastard that sold it to me was gone, moved-on and I never saw her again.

"Another thing: Never pay the asking price for anything. Everything is open for negotiation. If you pay them their asking price you will 'loose face' and be thought of as some kind of idiot. They'll say nasty stuff about you. In fact, when we get there, let me do all the talking. Just kind of hang-out and watch."

"How do you know that they'll be there?" Kevin asked.

"Someone will be there. Its like they have to come. They're attracted to money like moths to a flame. GIs get paid every month and have cash money. All of that money is stuck at the firebase with GIs who have no place to spend their dough. Besides, for the Vietnamese, it's a safe place to work. Sure, they might rob each other; even play a petty con on the GIs. But, while they're hangin' outside the firebase gate, real bandits aren't able to touch them. Some of the merchants are probably Viet Cong. You know, checking out the strength of our defenses. Still, it's a good thing to have them there."

"Why in the hell would any commander let enemy spies hang-out right outside their gate?" Kevin asked.

"They aren't all spies. These people are dependent on us, and not just to sell us stuff either. I've watched their little kids go into the garbage dumps and fight over the slop that the cooks throw-out. They're starving. The most important thing is, when they're not there; it is almost a sure sign that an attack is going to happen. The Vietnamese know when the enemy is around and they don't want to be caught in the crossfire."

We arrived at the firebase, checked in with the command center and actually did some 'official correspondent' business before heading outside the gate. Kevin got some interviews on tape and I shot some generic photographs. After all, we couldn't go back to the PIO empty-handed. We had plenty of time; the return chopper wasn't scheduled until three.

About two-dozen Vietnamese highway vendors had assembled at the side of the road fifty yards from the gate. The bazaar was bustling with activity. Traffic whizzed by on the highway. A few GIs wandered among a crowd. The customers were mostly Vietnamese travelers who had taken a break. The majority of customers had pulled off of the busy highway to stop for lunch. Altogether, more than fifty people were milling about checking-out all sorts of items that were offered for sale.

Some entrepreneurs arrived on bicycles, some had come on motorbikes and three-wheeled pedaled vehicles. The three-wheelers were like light weight carryall trucks. In Saigon, human powered versions of these tri-cycles had a seat between the front two wheels and were used as taxis. These tri-cycles had a cooler on the front axle and may have once been human powered ice cream trucks. While stationary, the tops of the coolers served as display counters for cigarettes and food. Some of the boxy metal coolers contained ice for drinks.

Kevin and I bought some beer. While we discussed the merits of Bam Nee Ba, I casually asked the barkeep if there was anyone selling pot in this open-air market. The beer seller pretended to not understand what I was asking. While feinting ignorance he pointed toward some waist-high black tents at the far end of the marketplace.

Kevin and I moseyed toward the tents. Surely, some of the tents had "Short Time Girls" (hookers) working inside. To avoid a potentially embarrassing situation, Kevin and I loudly announced ourselves outside a tent and waited for a summons to enter. No invitation was extended at the first tent we tried. Our luck improved on next attempt; a female voice beckoned us to enter.

We crawled, on our hands and knees, out of the glaring sun into the relative cool shaded interior of a black gauzy fabric shelter. Two women confronted us. One was young and pleasant looking; the other was neither attractive nor friendly. They were both squatting, rear ends inches off the ground, in a flat-footed position, that only Asian people considered comfortable. I knelt and sat on my heels directly across from the older woman. Her teeth were black from chewing Betel nut and she had an almost flat conical straw hat resting on the back of her head. Kevin sat, cross-legged, slightly behind me and was furthest away from the young lady on the old woman's right.

The old woman spoke first, in Vietnamese, while her partner translated. "What can we do for you gentlemen today?"

"We are looking to buy some marijuana." I said.

Apparently *marijuana* didn't translate well. I was forced to search for a synonym that our hosts understood. "Weed" turned out to be the right substitute. Momma-san reached into a large cloth bag, pulled out several plastic bags, selected one that had several tubes of rolled-up newspaper. She offered it to me for examination. I un-rolled the paper to find that contained a substantial quantity of the object of our quest. I passed it back for Kevin's approval. He remembered not to speak and, instead, gave me an approving nod accompanied by a big grin. I inquired about the cost of the package.

"Ten green U.S. dollars." Was the answer that came from the translator.

That may have been an excellent price back in the states. Nonetheless, I started to leave and apologized for taking-up the Momma-san's time. She gestured for me to stay and asked why I was in such a hurry to leave. I explained, I hadn't seen *American Greenbacks* since I had left the United States. This was true; in fact, possession of real U.S. currency was a jail-able offense. However, I would gladly pay her in Vietnamese Piasters.

Her reply was a grudging willingness to accept ten dollars MPC (Military Payment Certificates) for the amount of weed we wished to purchase. The game was afoot.

Now it was my turn to counter her offer. I said that a weed that grows wild along the side of the road and was only worth two hundred Piasters (two dollars Vietnamese).

The old woman wearing black silk pajamas pretended to be insulted, extolled the quality of her merchandise and said that she would take no less than eight dollars MPC.

I said that I really was willing to negotiate. But 400 Piasters was a fair price. Current exchange rate made Piasters worth about 80% of MPC.

The old lady was really getting worked up. The speed of her speech increased and the pitch of her voice rose. The translator was becoming uncomfortable.

I said that I thought that I was dealing with an *honorable* woman. Nonetheless, what plant, much less one growing wild all over Vietnam, could possibly be worth more than 600 Piasters?

The woman began to rant that I was a number 10 GI (the lowest on a scale where number one was best) and that I had a mustache that made my mouth look like the part of a water buffalo located just under its tail. I understood her entire rant without the services of her translator.

That was it! I lifted off of my heels, reached into the left leg pocket of my fatigue pants and pulled out my M2 paratrooper model carbine. I simultaneously extracted a thirty round clip from my right leg pocket. The women watched in horror as I slapped the magazine home. Holding the now loaded weapon in my right hand, I reached into my left upper pants pocket, produced one five dollar MPC note and dramatically slapped it down next to the rolled paper that held the weed. Staring directly into the Momma-san's eyes I whispered, "That is my final offer!"

The old woman didn't flinch or hesitate. She snapped-up my money.

I said, "Come Co Che (Vietnamese for '*Thank You Mam*')". I then spent a moment; re-rolling the newspaper, stashing it in a pocket, removing the magazine from my carbine and putting it away as well. My focus never wandered from my hostess. Kevin and I began to leave.

The old woman said, in perfect English, "Please don't go. Stay and have tea with me."

I said that we would be honored to have tea with her. We returned to our places and watched as the Momma-san slid a tray, that seemed to "materialize" from some obscure corner, into the center of the cramped space. The tray had a teapot and a stack of dainty cups that were designed without handles. The cups were filled and passed around.

During the chopper ride, back to Lai Khe, I assured Kevin that I never had any intention of shooting the old lady back in the tent. Pulling my weapon was just negotiation theatrics. I pointed-out that I hadn't actually chambered a round and, without doing that, no one could have been shot.

Kelly returned to his tent with basic negotiating skills, along with the last bag of pot that I bought during my year-long tour in Vietnam. I didn't see much of Kevin after that. Apparently, he was only interested in my procurement skills and dumped me, as a friend. I was grateful for no longer being involved. Teaching Kelly how to buy pot was kind of fun; in a 'black-market' sort of way.

The last time I saw Kevin Kelly, he was the center of attention in a formation called to award him an Army Commendation Medal. His citation was read before a group gathered to applaud his outstanding dedication to duty. The award specifically lauded Kelly's fortitude "*while facing perils in his pursuit of broadcast journals.*" I smiled, believing Kevin was really being awarded a medal for his quest to find something to roll into a joint and smoke. The biggest potential peril Kevin faced was being lucky to not have suffered a severe cough or unquenchable case of the munchies.

GRASSHOPPER

G rasshopper came to the Public Information Office fresh from the stateside Correspondent School at Fort Benjamin Harrison. He was an Army trained 71 Q 20 correspondent. That was his designation, job and military destiny.

Grasshopper's moniker could be attributed to the TV program **Kung Fu**. The show, broadcast over Armed Forces Vietnam Network (AFVN) Saigon, came to us on the office's black and white set. *You have so much to learn Grasshopper*, was the often-repeated theme on the show and seemed appropriate for this naive replacement.

From the moment Grasshopper walked through the door he earnestly aspired to make a *meaningful contribution*.

Only a couple of days after his arrival, Grasshopper decided his war winning contribution would be more "meaningful" if it was made on the battlefield. The rookie didn't want to just witness and report on the fighting. He wanted to actively participate. It wasn't a case of his being morbidly curious, having a death wish or a desire to kill anyone. Grasshopper just wanted to "put his money where his mouth was." Honesty was the motivating force for this tall, lanky kid wearing oversized GI eyeglasses. He had no weapons training. He had no physical training after Basic. Grasshopper had no clue. Grasshopper wanted to transfer to a combat unit.

Granting Grasshopper's request for a transfer to a line unit would have been the same as sentencing him to death.

This Private supported the war. Grasshopper recognized that there was a big job to be done and he wanted to be involved. Bill Johanson, Bob Mancini, Tony Hallas and myself had served with line units. Each of us proudly wore a CIB (Combat Infantry Badge). So, Grasshopper came to each of us, individually, soliciting our help. He wanted us to help him hatch some kind of scheme that would have him transferred out of the PIO.

Grasshopper was like a salmon going up stream. He was trying to rush into a burning building. No one was willing to help him. As a group, we collectively expressed our concerns to Sergeant First Class Stevenson. Perhaps, after this tour, he could re-up and become a Marine?

Sergeant First Class Stevenson, in his Solomon-like wisdom, offered Grasshopper an alternative. He presented Grasshopper the position of **dispatch messenger**; the recently vacated position that had been held by Perez (the same Puerto Rican Private who had suggested that I learn to speak Vietnamese). We conspired to convince Grasshopper by dramatizing the real dangers of driving anywhere in Vietnam. Lai Khe was thirty-five miles north of Saigon. Grasshopper would use the office's Jeep, to drive to the First Division PIO branch office in Di An. He would pick-up and deliver paperwork to USARVN (United States Army Vietnam) Headquarters and/ or Military Assistance Command Vietnam (MACV) in Saigon. As Dispatch Messenger he would deliver journalistic submissions.

It was risky work, involving driving in convoys, in an open jeep. The Vietnamese traveled the road on everything ranging from ox-carts to diesel trucks. Most of the traffic moved on two wheels; no one was licensed or had the vaguest comprehension of rules of the road. *There were no rules. There were no cops.* Vietnamese drivers were unpredictable to the point of suicidal. There was also a real possibility of being ambushed. Grasshopper would wear a Steel Pot, flack jacket and was issued his own personal M-16. Dispatch Messenger was not usually somebody with a correspondent's MOS (Military Occupational Specialty). Grasshopper thrived on the job. He exchanged his innocent gullibility for macho, developed a swaggering gait and quit hanging around with the correspondents. Sometimes he would not wait for the formation of a convoy and cruise the highway solo.

He became a lone knight speeding along Vietnam's most dangerous highway.

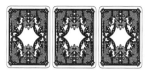

REMFs REMEMBERED

W orking in the rear echelon was somewhat safer, but provided no guarantee of sanctuary. REMFs were exposed to snipers, enemy rockets and terrorists. Their odds of becoming a casualty might have been less than those of an infantryman out in the jungle but they were still vulnerable.

Some of the most overlooked stories of the Vietnam War were accounts of Vietnamese people and their interactions with GIs. We were fighting the war, along with the Army of Vietnam troops–*to protect civilians*. Many Vietnamese depended on us to keep the Viet Cong terrorists away.

Spc. 5 Jack La Rocca, 1st Infantry Division 1st Admin Company checks a woman from Chanh Luu village as her child watches inquisitively.

I interviewed and photographed everyone: soldiers, men, women and children. Everyone had a story. I wanted to hear them all and separate fiction from truth; good from bad.

There was a lot of hyperbole and many out-right lies. Clerks told the scariest war stories . Real combat veterans simply didn't want to talk about it.

The medical corpsmen from the Headquarters, First Infantry Division 1st Admin Company held daily "Sick Call." They ministered to the clerks' rashes and bellyaches. REMF medics weren't involved with the level of gore and trauma that field medics saw. But they are "medics" and medics are motivated by a desire to help people. Naturally, the physical well-being of soldiers was their primary mission. But the "hearts and minds" of the Vietnamese were an important secondary objective. Our medics won Vietnamese hearts by giving them aid and comfort, often hundreds of time in the course of a day.

After they had met the needs of the GIs, headquarters medics often spent the rest of their day on humanitarian missions helping civilians in nearby villages. Occasionally, I went along to document their charitable efforts.

One night, the medic's tent took a direct hit by the very first 121-mm rocket in a surprise attack. It was a random shot that exploded before the warning sirens had started.

All of the medics were killed.

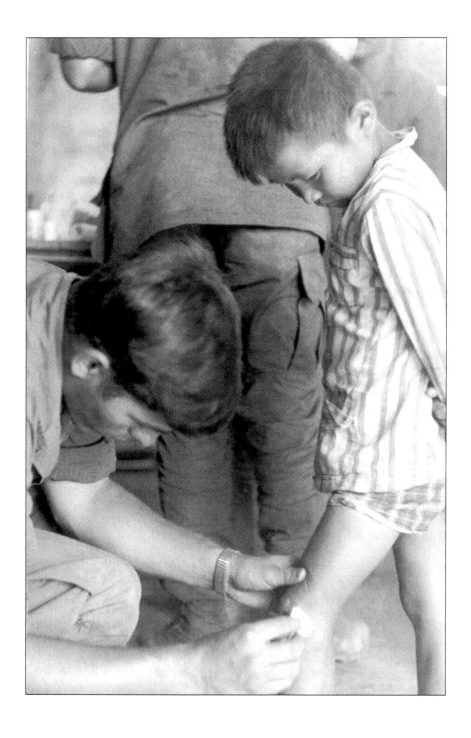

THE INDIFFERENT

VIETNAMESE

Perez the dispatch messenger (not the same sleepy Perez from Bandido Charlie) piqued my curiosity. He was the Dispatch Messenger who preceded Grasshopper. His experiences inspired me to learn about the Vietnamese people.

Perez was a short-timer when we met, meaning he had almost finished with his tour and was ready return to his native Puerto Rico. I had been out in the boonies of Vietnam and had just transferred into the PIO. Listening to people's stories had already become my personal mission. Perez told about his exploits in Saigon and his unauthorized, after curfew, visits into the village of Lai Khe.

I was naturally cynical about Perez's stories. Following the money, I questioned the Private First Class about his having the financial where-with-all to spend so much time in Saigon's bars and brothels. Perez explained that, as far as money went, he spent almost nothing. Furthermore, he sent most of his pay home. It was his explanation, for why money was not required, that really stirred my interest. He explained that by keeping an open mind, about the Vietnamese people, he learned a lot and had fun, as well.

Perez said that by spending time, instead of money, he had developed an understanding of the civilians that everyone else had simply overlooked. The dispatch driver claimed that listening and paying attention, as opposed to using the locals, had supplied him with a better education than reading books. He found that first-hand knowledge was way better than accepting someone else's opinion. Showing the Vietnamese some respect and learning to speak even a tiny amount of Vietnamese had taught him that the people of

Vietnam had huge amounts of heart, were extremely generous and immensely kind. His views went counter to the prevailing stereotype.

The best way to find out, if Perez was telling the truth, was by trying to replicate his exploits. Unfortunately, Perez was leaving. He couldn't teach me Vietnamese, take me to the places he had gone to or introduce me to anyone he had gotten to know. Additionally, I had to unlearn some behaviors and break some bad habits. Dehumanizing the enemy is the tradition method of rationalizing murdering them. It is difficult to kill someone if you think of them as someone's son or brother. We were encouraged to refer to the local people as *gooks*, *dinks* or *slopes*. It was as though institutional bigotry was encouraged.

That maybe fine in the infantry, but I had to stop thinking that way if I really wanted to hears people's stories. I also had to find someone willing to tutor me in the local language and customs. Even though I saw Vietnamese people all around me, my choices for instructors were limited.

The girl who cleaned my hooch and did my laundry wouldn't do. She barely spoke enough English to ask for her pay. The lady barber, whom I had a tremendous crush on, was too busy. I asked the lady who ran the gift shop, next door to the photo lab, to teach me how to say *hello* in Vietnamese. She broke into a big smile and eagerly agreed to help me. This incredibly amicable young woman encouraged me to learn as much as she could teach.

To my amazement, the Vietnamese word for *hello* was exactly the same as the Italian *ciao*. It meant *hello* and *goodbye* in Vietnamese just like it does in the language of my ancestors. The infantry had taught words like *halt*, *come here* and *surrender*. I wanted to learn less threatening phrases like *please* and *thank you*" My biggest linguistic breakthrough came when my instructor taught me to sing in Vietnamese.

Vietnamese is a tonal language. In Vietnamese, inflection and tone are linked to syntax and vocabulary. It takes more than just knowing the correct word to speak Vietnamese. Inflection, how you say a word, has a huge bearing on the meaning of what is being said. My teacher wanted me to think of her language more like the lyrics of a song. Adding to the complexity: Asian people do not sing using the same eight note tonal scale that Westerners use. They have a totally different interpretation of musical concepts like harmony and cords.

Evidently, my instructor was also a romantic with a sense of humor. She picked two songs that were popular on civilian radio stations. One was a local version of a *Romeo and Juliette* with lyrics about a GI and Vietnamese girl. The GI went home, promising to return. The girl waited and became impatient, believing he wasn't coming back, she committed suicide. He eventually did return, discovered that she died and committed suicide. The song was a big hit in Vietnam and was similar to the theme used as a stage play in the States. I only learned the first verse of the song. That was enough. I would meet a Vietnamese person, claim that I wanted to learn more verses of the song and sing for them. Pretty soon people around me would join in and sing along with me. Everyone would wind-up laughing, singing and generally becoming friends. Perez was right. The Vietnamese people are some of the friendliest people on earth.

Culturally, there were so many things to learn. Beckoning for someone's attention is never done with the palm of the hand facing upwards. In Vietnam, that is the same as flipping someone off, regardless of what finger (or fingers) are employed. The gesture for someone to come, is done palm-down and using all four fingers.

The Vietnamese have developed their special brand of hegemony over centuries. Apparently all cultures, including the Vietnamese, have racial prejudices. They didn't like the Chinese. After friendly conversations with dozens, perhaps hundreds, of Vietnamese people I learned their views on history and current events.

Historically, Vietnam has always been one of a very few places in Asia capable of growing more rice than its people could consume. China had invaded Vietnam, and stolen, this precious resource countless times over many millennial. These serial invasions forced the Vietnamese to evolve a patient strategy of relentless resistance. They developed effective weapons and used attrition to drive the Chinese away every time. Some might say that the Vietnamese were the world's original insurgents.

Initially, when France picked Indochina for its foray into empire building, the Vietnamese exhibited tolerance. The French introduced Catholic Christianity, technology and global capitalistic commerce to Vietnam. Unlike China, France didn't simply steal the population's food. The French developed new revenue steams, mainly in rubber, and re-invested some of their profits back into the country. Saigon was transformed, from an Asian backwater, into a flourishing tropical metropolis. Saigon flourished and earned the title "Paris of the Orient."

Japan invaded Vietnam during WWII. The Vietnamese hated the Japanese even more than their traditional enemy the Chinese. During WWII, Ho Chi Minh negotiated a deal with the French. His people would help the French drive out the Japanese invaders out of Vietnam in return for his country becoming a commonwealth. Ho saw post-war Vietnam as less of a French colony and more of an independent nation, with equitable trade agreements. The French agreed. But, when the war was over, and time came for the French to keep their word, France double-crossed Ho Chi Minh. France only released the North half of the country. The French wanted to keep the rice-rich Mekong Delta, rubber plantations and the beautiful (Paris of the Orient) Saigon. Ho Chi Minh was not happy. *Who could he turn to?* Ho had been an U.S. ally during the war against Japan. But, he was aware of the historic ties between the United States and France. He knew that he couldn't ask the United States for help in his fight for independence from the French. Therefore Ho Chi Minh had no other choice and was forced to turn to his ancient enemy, China, for assistance. He, once again, became an insurgent. The French paid for their treachery in human lives.

It isn't clear whether we wanted to avenge the embarrassing loss of our French ally or that the United States believed its own hype about a 'Cold War Domino Theory.' The United States invented a pretext and sent troops to defend a puppet government it had set-up in Saigon. We became mired a civil war that should never have happened and wound-up fighting people that had once been our friends.

The people of North Vietnam loved Ho Chi Minh, South Vietnam, at the very least, respected him. Ho was the father of their country a George Washington figure. Ho Chi Minh died on September 2, 1969, roughly a month before I was scheduled to leave Vietnam. Everyone was anticipating a huge violent offensive commemorating the departed leader. The Tet Offensive had resulted in thousands of deaths only eighteen months earlier. Now, Ho Chi Minh had passed and...*nothing happened*. There was no escalation. The war just continued to grind-on at the same pace. No big thing, apparently the enemy had shot their wad at Tet. They had nothing left. The spin that was promoted held that VC and the North Vietnamese were hanging-on by their fingernails. Our enemy was on the verge of defeat.

The reality was that the bad guys didn't have to win battles. All they had to do was hang-on. They had done this kind of thing for centuries and could continue to do it indefinitely. Pham Van Dong, the North Vietnamese Prime Minister was totally sincere, back in 1966, when he said, "How long do you Americans want to fight? One year? Two years? Three years? Five years? Ten years? Twenty years? We will be glad to accommodate you." Dong's strategy was as ancient as it was straightforward. Unfortunately, we simply did not have a meaningful counter-strategy.

Every Vietnamese I interviewed knew that we would have to leave some day. The South Vietnamese were nice people. They enjoyed all the money we were spending. The death, chaos and destruction that we were heaping upon Vietnam were only a temporary diversion from whatever long-range plan fate held. Eventually we were going to have to leave and they were going to stay. We were destructive visitors, obnoxious guests, who had overstayed our welcome. In the end, it was their country.

A strange realization became manifestly apparent: many Vietnamese were, at best, benignly indifferent to our intervention in their domestic struggle.

LETTERS FROM THE DARK SIDE

G.I's in The 1st Air Cavalry Division!

Christmas an ♂ New Year have come!

Without your presence under the familiar Xmas tree, how much worried and longing for you your dear ones at home are! Yet, in the mean time you are being kept in deserted jungles shadowed by danger and death in this remote country of Vietnam!

Why and for whom you are ten thousand miles from home, do you know?

It is the Washington Administration which has deceived and compelled you to go over here. You are not fighting for Freedom but for the repression and slaughter of the Vietnamese people who are struggling for Peace, Independence and Freedom.

Is it conceivable that you are unaware of the fact that your blood is being shed in defence of the selfish interest of the war-like capitalists in the White House and the Pentagon and to save the Saigon puppet running-dogs who are abhorred and condemned by all Vietnamese people?

You usually pray for an early restoration of Peace so that you can soon get into a homebound ship.

But first and foremost you must take action.

G.I's, resolutely oppose the illegal, immoral and unjust war of Washington; demand that the US Government ends the war at once and restores peace in South Vietnam; let the Vietnamese people settle their own affairs themselves.

By doing so, can you preserve the honor of America, can you rejoin your families for the coming Christmas and New Year in Peace and Happiness.

Disseminating effective propaganda was not one of our adversary's strong points. Historically, the Vietnamese people had dealt with invaders for centuries and may have been among the world's earliest insurgent fighters. The North Vietnamese and Viet Cong were extremely efficient at killing, maiming and injuring their enemies. However, their twentieth century attempts at persuasive writing were, at best, awkward and clumsy.

G.I's IN THE 1st AIR CAVALRY DIVISION !

Isn't it that the drumfire of fierce attack of the Liberation Armed Forces in the Quang-tri—Thua-thien battlefield still resounds unto you ? Is it that the scene of thousands of casualty of cavalrymen and 350 choppers shot down or destroyed there hasn't blurred out from your memory ?

Yet, at the time being Abrams has driven you down here to Eastern Nam-bo, the upmost burning theatre of operation.

As you all know, it is in this battlefield that tens of thousand of G.I's were put out of combat, and all such biggest operations of the U.S Forces as Attleboro and Junction City were frustrated in the 1966—1967 dry season.

It is in this battlefield that in the last 2 months, Aug. and Sept., the reinforced 1st Bde, 25th Inf. Div. was knocked out of action, more than ten thousand G.I's were killed or wounded including Lieutenant General Keith Ware, the «Big Red One» Commander.

It is in this battlefield too, shortly after your arrival here, you came under successive attacks of the L.A.F in the areas of Suoi-ngo, Soc Con-trang and Thien-ngon (Tay-ninh). Hundreds of cavalrymen in your division were killed or wounded in these actions.

CAVALRYMEN IN THE 1ST AIRMOBILE DIVISION !

For what aim did Abrams transfer you to this battlefield of Eastern Nam-bo, whereas a great number of G.I's in the 1st and 25th Inf. Divisions are staging struggles against raiding operations, for withdrawal of troops home ? Isn't it that your coming here is to shoulder the Danger and Death which Abrams and the other units wish to shift onto you !

Can it be that you submit to Abrams and the U.S Generals to make you a pawn on the gambit ? Is it reasonable for you to let yourselves be driven down a senseless and useless death while you have all means available for your survival ?

YOUR LIVES AND THE WISH OF EARLY HOME RETURN FOR FAMILY REUNION SPUR YOU TO:

— DEMAND THAT THE US GOVERNMENT STOP THE WAR AND RESTORE PEACE IN VIETNAM !

— REFUSE TO GO OUT ON OPERATION, TO TERRORIZE AND MASSACRE THE VIETNAMESE PEOPLE WHO ARE STRUGGLING FOR INDEPENDENCE AND PEACE.

— DEMAND THE WITHDRAWAL OF U.S TROOPS HOME, LET THE VIETNAMESE PEOPLE SETTLE THEIR OWN AFFAIRS ! G.I's, DON'T DIE THE WORTHLESS DEATH OF THE LAST MAN IN THE LAST BATTLE IN VIETNAM.

These almost laughably crude leaflets, were the enemy's counter attempt at winning the "Hearts and Minds" of the Vietnamese people. (The flip-side of these leaflets were printed in Vietnamese.) Their false bravado and shameless exaggeration was more taunting than telling. These pathetically poorly written prose were more inspiration for finding their author, and putting him out of his misery, than converting American soldiers to their political position.

MENTORS

The First Infantry Division Public Information Office was located in a large tent on edge of the Division Headquarters campus in 1968. The photographic darkroom occupied one relatively small corner of a large rectangular empty warehouse building across the street just East of the Division Headquarters complex. Early in 1969 the warehouse was converted into offices. The Judge Advocate, American Red Cross and the Public Information Office moved out of their tents and into the corrugated metal building. The darkroom

Seamstress, Barber, me and unknown associate behind their shop in Lai Khe.

stayed in the warehouse building, where it had always been, while the Public Information Office materialized around it.

A cream-colored stucco building sat next-door to the new office. The combination Barbershop, Gift Emporium and Seamstress Shop had a red tiled roof. Two Vietnamese women operated the three businesses. They were friends. Our neighbors tutored me in local customs, helpful phrases and Vietnamese music.

These songs, coupled a sincere interest and a willingness to learn made me kind of unique among GI's. My curiosity about in Vietnamese culture exposed me to a warm and generous side of the citizenry that few soldiers were able to explore. I thanked my Vietnamese teachers with photographs. They shared my pictures with their friends and family.

These two women also taught me Vietnamese history from a more local perspective. They also shared their views on current affairs. My barber/language-coach came from Chinese ancestry. She explained how local custom segregated her from native Vietnamese. The Cholon district of Saigon, known for the biggest Post Exchange in the country, was also a ghetto for people of Chinese descent.

Our barber was the proud owner of the only mini-dress in Lai Khe.

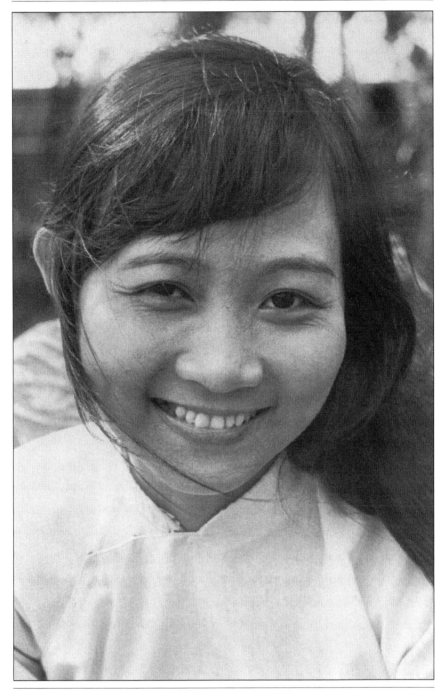

Seamstress and Gift Shop owner. Her business was located next door to the Public Information Office, one block away from 1st Infantry Division Headquarters.

Vietnamese interpreter working with the US Military Police at a checkpoint going into Lai Khe.

ORPHANS

Anthropologists in Vietnam during 1969 would have seen a society with some unusual anomalies.

The most obvious abnormality was the absence of healthy men between the ages of sixteen and fifty years old. Those guys just weren't around. Members of this demographic group had either been killed, drafted by their government and/or kidnapped by the Viet Cong or North Vietnamese. Therefore, almost all able-bodied adult males were absent, simply missing from the general population.

Amazingly, there was still an abundance of children. Even more remarkably, a disproportionate number of those kids appeared to be boys. The kids on page 195, running on the tops of desks in an empty school were following me. To them, I was the Pied Piper in olive drab fatigues. They were chasing me for some hard candy. I brought candy along with me as a reward for their participating in a chase/tag game we played when I visited the village of Lai Khe. The boys on page 70, on the other hand, are reaching for a cigarette held just out of their reach. Boys started smoking at the tender age of six.

Boys traveled in packs, begging and stealing for survival, smoking cigarettes and running wild like escapees from William Golding's Lord of the Flies. There was little concern about the long-term effect of nicotine on theses little guys' health because they didn't have much of a "life expectancy" anyway.

Little girls were generally kept out of sight or, as in the photo on page 197, confined to their yard behind a barbed wire fence. Those kids were probably smiling because their masonry house was considerably more substantial than the corrugated shed where the bewildered little boy on page 198 lived. His work-from-home mother is ironing laundry in the shade of their open door. The Hunt's Tomato soup can nailed to their door post contained a candle that served as their porch light. Tropical temperatures with high humidity were contributing factors for uniformly short haircuts and clothing optional dress illustrated by the mature beyond their years young men posing for a portrait, below.

In Lai Khe, school's out completely.

Burn victim waiting to see medics.

THE UNGRATEFUL

GOING HOME

Coincidence, *a very strange coincidence*, compelled me to volunteer for the draft two weeks before the Tet Offensive. Another strange coincidence occurred when I extended my one-year tour in Vietnam two weeks before Ho Chi Minh's death. Luckily, neither of these unusual happpenstances resulted in disastrous consequences.

Mere gossip, speculation really, inspired me to extend my year-long tour of duty in Vietnam. *The rumor was*: if a soldier had less than five months active duty left on his military commitment when he returned from Vietnam, the Army would discharge him. It was rumor. There was no official memo, nothing in writing. It could have been a hoax. I had volunteered for the draft because being drafted required only two years active duty, enlisting would have meant four years active duty. My tour of duty was finished in October. I had been drafted in March. I knew that I still had some "active duty" time left. An honorable discharge from the Army had always been my goal. If two additional weeks in Vietnam would expedite my ultimate goal, it was essential that I explore that option.

When exactly had I officially become an integral part of the Army? Was it the day I reported to the draft board? Was it the day, a couple of days later, when I took the oath? What was the precise date? And I had crossed the International Date Line on the way in Vietnam, what bearing would that have upon my remaining time? I had no way of knowing **exactly** how much time I would have left in the service when I got back. I didn't even have my return orders yet. But, if I waited until I had my orders, it would probably be too late to put in a request for an extension.

I had nightmares about standing in front of some stateside clerk and hearing him say, "You have just over five months active duty left. Sorry, we have got to draw the line somewhere. Here are your orders for Fort Polk. For the next five months and one week you will be training troops headed for Vietnam." It was a nightmare that I couldn't let happen. So, I requested that my tour of duty, in Vietnam, be extended by two weeks.

I was not the only GI who had heard the rumor about a five-month-early-out.

My two-week extension had been granted. On the revised date in October, I donned my Class A Summer Uniform (spit shined dress shoes, khaki pants, short sleeve shirt with the appropriate ribbons, patches, rank and name tag) and headed for Long Binh. **The day I had waited one year and two weeks for had finally come**. I was going to process-out and board a plane back to the real world. I carried an AWOL bag (gym bag to civilians) with my paperwork. The same duffel bag that I was issued at Ft. Knox was slung over my shoulder. I joined the final check-out line.

I could not *believe* my eyes.

Terry Wise was standing in line ten feet in front of me!

The same Terry Wise who had traveled with me from Fort Knox to Fort Polk to Fort Benning. The same Terry Wise who had gotten drunk with me in Leesville and Phenix City. The exact same Terry Wise who had gone through basic, AIT and dropped-out of NCO School. The same Terry Wise whom I met at Fort Dix and flown to Vietnam with. Yes, **T-H-A-T** Terry Wise!

Terry had heard the same rumor I had heard, extended his tour two weeks (just like I had) and was going to fly back to the WORLD sitting in the seat next to me, just like he had on all those other flights.

It was in-*fucking*-credible!

When Terry and I had gone our separate ways, one year and two weeks ago, each of us had been assigned to our different units. Terry had gone south to the Ninth Division, and I had gone north to the First Infantry Division. Neither of us had specific addresses, we weren't able to write. There was no way I could have told Terry about the five-month-early-out rumor or that I was going to extend my tour. Seeing him in line was incredible. There he was, as if he had somehow known my plan.

After a huge amount of hand shaking and backslapping, Terry traded places with the guy in front of me. We shared our amazement, at seeing one another, and immediately began to catch-up on our individual experiences. Terry Wise and I were old friends re-united.

Processing the paperwork for leaving Vietnam went much more quickly than the exercise of coming into Vietnam. This one time, the seemingly infinite methodology involved in *hurrying up to wait* did not apply.

Our flight slipped past fairly quickly. It felt like old times, Terry and I seated on still another chartered airliner ready for take-off. This time, everyone on board cheered when the plane's wheels left the ground. Our collective excitement and the stamping of all the passenger's feet shook the airliner. We were finally leaving— *going home at last!*

Apprehension, about our unknown future, had morphed into nervous tension that kept us awake on our flight to Vietnam. Now, relaxed conversation and the relief of having dodged fate's cruel possibilities would keep us awake on our way home.

Terry and I had taken a northern route to arrive in Vietnam. This time we would follow an equally tedious southerly course. We stopped in Guam and Honolulu before landing in San Francisco. We were bused over to Oakland Army Base to play *hurry up and wait* for the last time.

Once again Terry and I parted. This time Terry was headed for Louisville and I was going to Detroit. Just like the last time we parted company, we promised to meet at the Zansza Bar in Louisville.

The flight had taken almost twenty-four monotonous hours. We had crossed back over the International Date Line, had no clue about how long it would take to be separated from the Army and were subjected to the uncertainties associated with traveling on domestic military standby. With that vagueness in mind, I had been intentionally imprecise, to my family. I rationalized that it would be better to surprise my mother and sisters than have some public display in an airline terminal. Besides, there was no way to know the exact time that I would arrive home. After being bumped off of a direct flight, I caught another with a layover in St. Louis.

In order to surprise my mother and sisters, I phoned my old friend Gordon during my layover in St. Louis. Gordie was the same friend I had killed time with while hanging out during the last week of my only Army leave. Before I left for Vietnam, we had loitered in a bar on Eight Mile Road and watched the World Series. Now I was calling him, asking him to meet me at Detroit Metropolitan Airport for a ride home.

Gordon Munn was waiting for me at the gate. It was so good to see my old high school friend. There was much hand shaking and back clapping. Gordie had not brought along his family. His wife was home with their children. Technically, no one else knew that I was in Detroit. No one was expecting to see me, or, to show-up at any specific time. It had been over a year since I had had any American food.

I was hungry, to the point of craving, for a *good old fashioned* greasy hamburger. My hunger for real (not re-constituted and packaged in a can) French fries had almost become a desperate desire. We decided to stop on our way to my mother's house.

One hamburger, fries and a beer led to another beer and several more beers. *We were celebrating.* We bought still more beer and continued to celebrate.

It was after dark when we reached my mother's house. I was deliberately loud pounding on mom's back door. It didn't take long to get her attention, as well as the attention of all of our neighbors. Our celebratory mood infected several households. There was a fairly large impromptu party.

Gordie got a phone call from his wife just when I thought my surprise homecoming had worked-out to be about as good as I had anticipated it would. Joe Lovell had just come home from Vietnam. He was at the airport and needed a ride home.

Roseville is on the east side of Detroit. Metropolitan Airport is so far west of Detroit that it is actually closer to Ann Arbor than

Detroit. Normally, the drive from Roseville to the airport would have taken more than an hour. It was late, there was no traffic or cops. Somehow, Gordie and I made the journey in just over twenty minutes. The airport was just as deserted as the highway had been.

Drunk and uncertain about exactly where we could find Joe, Gordie and I shouted his name as we wandered through the terminal. Astonishingly, we weren't arrested. Even more phenomenal was the fact that we found Lovell. Joe was sober. Gordon and I were not. That situation was rectified as we made a more leisurely return back to our hometown.

The really intense return home celebration only lasted for a *couple of days*. Those happy times seemed to pass so quickly.

My appreciation for having survived and my returning home never stopped.

The party mode gradually lessened and eventually leveled off.

I had so much to be grateful for at a time when gratitude was in short supply.

News of the My Lai Massacre broke within two weeks of my homecoming in 1969. The actual massacre had happened on March 16, 1968, coincidently very near the same time that I had began my Army career. Troops from C Company (1st BN, 20th Infantry Reg. 11th Brigade) 23rd Infantry Division had killed every man woman and child in the village of My Lai. The people of that coastal town in Vietnam's Central Highlands had been harboring Viet Cong guerillas. To say that our soldiers *over-reacted* would be understatement.

It was a horrible, indefensible, atrocity.

But, war is one huge atrocity.

I had been there and had seen many egregious behaviors. From personal experience, I can testify that our enemies were far more barbarous those men in the 23rd Division or; even the South Koreans. Some say the North Vietnamese Army (NVA) was a worthy adversary and describe the Viet Cong local as insurgents. In reality, the Viet Cong were primarily terrorists. They murdered and tortured civilians with impunity. Both enemy elements regularly bayoneted wounded soldiers. Neither the NVA or the Cong took prisoners. They were constantly on the run, had no place or provisions, and simply killed soldiers, wounded or not.

My Lai was the site of one American atrocity. Our adversaries committed atrocities on a nearly daily schedule. My Lai was wrong. It was bad. However, it was not a surprising event. There was no excuse for what the soldiers of the Americal Division had done. By the same token, what happened at My Lai should not have been used as an excuse to paint all of our soldiers with a wide brush and label them *baby killers*.

Yet, that is exactly what happened.

Screwed again.

The Tet Offensive had been twisted into a loss and now this incident was used to make all GIs look pathetic.

There are people, within my family, who still describe Vietnam veterans with that pejorative term.

DEAR SWEET MOTHER

As I progressively returned to my old routine, I found myself gravitating more toward old friends than family. That was attributable, in large part, to my mother's rigid agenda. Mother still insisted that I had to get a job and support her. That was not going to happen. I had rejected that course of action before I had volunteered for the draft and I saw no reason to accept it now. Mom was not pleased. She expressed her dissatisfaction endlessly to anyone who would listen. The welcoming embrace of my aunts, uncles and cousins cooled.

While I was in Vietnam, I had ordered a car though the PX. It was to have been a brand new 1970 Camaro convertible with a four-speed transmission and the largest engine available. As luck would have it, General Motors stopped making the convertible version of Camaro that year. I canceled the pre-ordered car and bought a Plymouth Barracuda convertible from a local dealer.

I moved into a small apartment. Since, I had risked my life to be eligible for the GI Bill. So, I enrolled at Wayne State University.

My major field of study was journalism. Don Easter became my favorite instructor and mentor. Easter was also the City Desk Editor at the *Detroit News*.

Mr. Easter found a position for me to work, as a paid intern, at the *Detroit News*. I gravitated toward the paper's photographic department. This job provided access to a more *modern* photo lab than the darkroom my father had left behind in my mother's basement. I had access to the newest photo processing equipment, provided by the nation's largest evening circulation newspaper. I would be able to make my prize winning portfolio!

The image quality of the prints I had made in Vietnam suffered because I had made them using warm chemistry. The photographs

I had printed in Vietnam were grainy and had too much contrast. Incorrect chemistry temperature would not be a problem in the *Detroit News* darkroom. All I had to do was pick-up the negatives that I had sent home from Vietnam, bring them to work and spend one of my off days making prints. Then I could apply for a real job, with a wire service or a national magazine. I wanted to go back to Vietnam and show that we could still win the war.

My soon-to-be printed samples would be sharp, have proper contrast and be suitable for an award-winning portfolio. These were going to be the images that I was unable to submit for publication in the Army. They were *unsuitable* at the PIO because they were obvious violations of the *No Dead Dirty or Wounded* rule. These were my never-seen-before dramatic black and white pictures. I had mailed home strips of film that had already been processed into negatives because negatives were more stable than unprocessed film. Postal X-rays could potentially damage film. Negatives were impervious to damage from that form of inspection. I had given my *very special* negatives a detailed inspection and knew they were ready to print. The photographs from these negatives would be nothing like the delightful human-interest stories the PIO wanted.

The night of my homecoming, before I finally went to bed, I secured the box that contained my special negatives. These were paramount. I had literally risked my life to take some of those pictures. That first night home, before I had put away my uniform, I wrote **IMPORTANT! DO NOT DISCARD!** with a red marker on the top and sides of the box that housed my negatives. The box was about the same size as a shoe box and held Glassine sleeves containing negatives from about twenty rolls of film. I took the freshly labeled box down stairs, into my basement darkroom, and hid it behind some unopened cans of chemistry. It was out of sight on a hard-to-reach top shelf concealed in my private laboratory.

My mother and sisters never had an interest in photography. Since Dad left, I was the only person in my family who used the darkroom. No one else knew how to operate the equipment. I hadn't told anyone where I had hidden my prized negatives.

While still living at home, mom had enlisted my help in cleaning-out 'stuff.' Dad had been an art teacher and left behind dozens of cans of powdered tempera paint in a rainbow of colors. He also left a wide range of craft supplies for making ceramics and jewelry. There was clay, modeling tools and several kilns of various types and sizes. All of it went into the trash. I gave most of his tools, as well as his Kennedy Tool Box, to Gordie. My Schwinn Phantom bicycle, in excellent condition, was placed on the curb. Everything, and there wasn't much, that I declared valuable and wanted to keep was placed in the darkroom.

The door was secured with a simple latch.

Now, I was finally ready to print my portfolio. I opened the darkroom door and switched on the light. All of the *valuable* equipment was exactly where I had left it. We had two photographic enlargers. I had stored my father's Rolliecord camera, a view camera and two Graphic press cameras on the shelves. The bottles, for storing liquid chemistry were under the sink. Brand new boxes of photographic paper, in a variety of sizes and surfaces, were right where I had recently put them. I stood on a small ladder, stretched to reach behind the cans of dry chemicals and felt for my hidden box of negatives.

It was not there.

I took everything off of the top shelf. No box. No negatives. Eventually, I took everything out of the darkroom. I completely emptied the darkroom. I searched every crack and crevice. I inventoried everything, returning every item to its original place. Everything that was supposed to be in the darkroom was in the darkroom.

Only one thing was missing: **THE box containing my special negatives.**

My mother was upstairs. I went to her, asked if she had seen the box with my negatives. She said that she had not seen such a box and claimed that she hadn't been inside the darkroom. I believed her. Mom could tell that I was upset. She seemed to be trying to placate me.

"Have you looked in your old bedroom closet? You have some stuff in there," she said.

The only thing that I had left in that closet should have been my dress uniform. The one I had worn when I came home. I looked in the closet. The box with my negatives was not in the closet. My dress uniform wasn't in the closet either. There was nothing that belonged to me in the closet. Rather than simply tell me that she had thrown out my dress uniform, my mother had sent me to the closet so I could discover, for myself, that my uniform along with my medals and battle ribbons were gone.

My anger was building from thunderstorm intensity to hurricane strength. Mom's plea of innocences were half-hearted and infuriating. She never said that my precious items must have been moved or misplaced. Mom never offered to help me find them. She hadn't offered to help because she knew what she had done. Mom was totally aware that my stuff would never be found.

My mother had deliberately sabotaged my plans. The person I trusted most, had betrayed me. I had told her of my plan to return to Vietnam. My mother had deliberately destroyed the negatives that were crucial to implementing my plan.

Now, my mother saw that her scheme had worked. She started toying with me. My mother was getting some kind of weird kick out of watching me become furious. Her intentional cruelty was achieving its desired effect. I became more livid as the realization that I was being played slowly dawned on me. ***My mother had destroyed my plan in retaliation for me, not supporting her!*** The emerging realization of her treachery was accompanied by a burgeoning desire to kill her. I had some experience killing people and I was familiar with the emotional place I needed to be in to make someone dead. I was there. I wanted her dead. My desire to do it was just as intense, as it was when I wanted to kill some faceless gook shooting at me out of a tree line.

At that very instant, when I realized my mother's deceit, I had an out-of-body experience. At the precise moment, when I became aware of an overpowering yearning to end my mother's life, time itself seemed to slip into slow motion. My viewpoint shifted and my consciousness moved out from behind my eyes. My auditory perception hovered somewhere nearby and I listened to my voice shouting like a lunatic. I heard my mother taunting me. She was daring me to kill her; like she didn't believe I had enough courage or she had some kind of death wish. My separated awareness remembered the *fight or flight* experience I had that first time a bullet whizzed past my ear. I had reached another cusp just like I had in Vietnam.

This time, new questions flashed through my mind: *Was I going to simply kill her with my bare hands?* What would happen if I just snapped her neck? Could I get away with it?

Would her death solve my problems? Or, would it create a whole new set of problems? How long would I be in jail? Would her death return my missing negatives? My out of body conscience deliberated, thinking of consequences for the horrific thing I was about to do.

Finally, I decided to just walk away.

The next thing I knew, I was driving away from my mother's house at an extreme rate of speed. I slowed down and thought about how close I had just come to killing my own mother.

For the next six months, my mother and I didn't speak. I probably would have been content to never speak to her again. But then, out of the blue mom phoned with her weak *apology*. It was a phony politician's generic *I'm sorry for whatever I may have done to upset you* apology. She never specifically said what she was apologizing for or what her motives may have been for doing it. Mom didn't even bother to say that she wouldn't do *whatever it was*, again. Of course, I forgave her. After all, she was my mother. There are several things that I could say about my mother, surprisingly most of them are very positive.

Here is my rationalization: My mother was *ungrateful*. She didn't know, care or appreciate where I had been or what I had done. It was not unusual for mom to not acknowledge my achievements. After all, they were my accomplishments, not hers. My mother had a very myopic point of view and it just happened to be an ungrateful viewpoint.

Mom wasn't the only person with unappreciative sentiments toward Vietnam Veterans. It appeared that the entire country had turned its back on its veterans. As the war dragged on, with no chance for *victory* in sight, more people were looking for someone to blame. Vietnam Veterans were taking that heat. After the My Lai massacre, we were *baby killers*.

There were rumors of war protesters spitting on Veterans. (That never happened to me.) Surprisingly, even the Veterans of Foreign Wars post in my hometown had bought into the country's ungracious hysteria. The VFW was not accepting Vietnam vets for membership. Being excluded from drinking cheap beer with WWII and Korean War vets really didn't matter. The insult of being intentionally excluded from Veterans' Day Parades mattered slightly. However, NOT honoring Vietnam Veterans who had made the ultimate sacrifice was inexcusable.

Perhaps it isn't so surprising that one of *my* sisters still claims that I killed babies in Asia.

At the time, I believed that the tide of support for the troops was draining away because no one was standing-up for us. I wanted to be one of the people supporting the troops and believed that, given the facts, more people would join me.

When I was in the fight, I believed that we couldn't lose. We out-gunned our enemy and consistently inflicted heavy losses on them. *I knew that we were winning*.

The enemy had never taken nor kept any territory. They had won no major battle. They were just hanging on. I wanted to go back to Vietnam and photographically show that our hard work and sacrifice was making a positive difference. Nice, positive, human-interest stories weren't going to cut it. I didn't want to be restrained by *no dead, dirty or wounded*. I had been there and done that. I wanted to send back positive proactive photographic proof that we were fighting the good fight and *winning*.

No longer having the photographic negatives for my war portfolio had been a major set back. Still, I had to set the record straight; before it was too late. I just had to make some new plans.

ART CHECH

I still had my job as a photographic copy-boy at the *Detroit News*. I was only an intern—a copy-boy. I mixed chemicals, mopped darkroom floors and delivered photographs to various editors throughout the newspaper. I needed some recognition as a photographer.

My new game plan occurred to me during one of my multiple circuits through the immense *Detroit News* building. The revised strategy: I would pitch one of the many editors I saw, on daily basis, with an idea for a photo story, have that story published and build a new portfolio. Then, I could use my new portfolio to get a job working for a newspaper or wire service as a photographer (not a copy-boy), go back to Vietnam and photograph the war from a perspective that was more supportive of the troops. I chose the editor of *The Other Section* for a feature story and approached him with my idea.

The *Detroit News* was the nation's largest evening circulation newspaper. Its demographic audience was 34-48 year olds, white working class. The *News* had a richly deserved reputation for being stodgy to the point of prosaic. Their competition, the *Detroit Free Press*, was winning the circulation war for a more desirable younger demographic. It published more trendy, happening, stories. The *News'* geriatric editorial staff searched for something to project a more 'hip' image and attract younger readers. *The Other Section* was created to reach the younger demographic. I developed a photo story idea that could be useful in reaching that elusive younger audience.

The *Detroit News* had hired a younger (compared to all the other editors) man and put him in charge of this new and contemporary part of the paper. The new section was titled *The Other Section* so it wouldn't be confused with all the other same old humdrum fish-wrap parts of the newspaper. *The Other Section* of the *Detroit News* was targeted at people like me. Therefore, *The Other Section*'s editor had to be the ideal candidate for my photo story concept.

I pitched my idea. *The Other Section* editor agreed that my proposal might have some merit. I was encouraged to bring in some photos. I shot the pictures on my own time, with film that I purchased. My images were produced after working hours. The *Other Section* editor liked my work. Six of my pictures were published on the back page. The editor insisted on paying me as well as attributing the photographs to me with photo credit byline. My friends phoned me with congratulations. The *Detroit News* staff photographers congratulated me.

My revised strategy appeared to be working.

I was summoned to Art Chech's office. Chech was the *Detroit News'* Photo Editor. His office was in an area completely separate from the Photo Department. The Photo Department supervisor assigned my daily tasks. Art Check was my supervisor's boss. I had often left prints of other photographer's work on his desk, but had never actually spoken to him. Now, he had specifically requested that I, the peon copy-boy, come to his office.

I took a short cut through the Photo Department. I could barely contain my excited anticipation as I threaded my way through the now-familiar maze of hallways and rooms that occupied most of an entire floor. I walked past multiple photo labs (occupied by full-time lab technicians), a spacious studio, prop and equipment rooms, additional rooms for sorting and drying prints and a special lounge area designated for staff photographers (when they weren't off on assignments).

This would be my big opportunity.

I lightly rapped on the Photo Editor's closed door. The door had a white-pebbled glass window with 'ART CHECH' painted on it. I was given permission to enter and told to close the door behind me. Art Chech, sitting at his desk, did not invite me to sit down. I stood, back to the door, looking down at the thinning white hair on the top of his head. Art Check was easily twice my age. A smoldering a cigarette was perched on the edge of an over-flowing ashtray sitting atop a pile of papers. The horizontal surface of Chech's desk was littered with paper, a coffee cup and photographs. Art Chech didn't looked up from the chaotic clutter on his desk. He made me stand there and wait.

Finally, Art Chech said the only words he would ever say to me: "You work in the Photographic Department of the *Detroit News*. You will never sell photographs to this newspaper. As of this moment you are officially fired. Now, get the hell out of my office."

That was all. There was no warning or discussion. I had been summarily dismissed.

A uniformed security guard escorted me from the building. There were no farewells. Twenty minutes ago, I had a job and plans for the future. Now, I was unemployed, standing beside Lafayette Avenue.

My first thought was to walk two blocks east on Lafayette, to the *Detroit Free Press*, and introduce myself to that Photo Editor. I had lots of experience; my photographs had been published all over the United States. I had even photographed President Nixon. I didn't even have tearsheets, much less a referral from anyone with a title in front of their name.

Art Chech was not going to give me a reference. The images that I had printed in Vietnam were not necessarily my best work because they were not *professional quality* photographs. So, despite everything I had done, I still had no real portfolio. The *Detroit Free Press* wasn't a realistic option.

The war in Vietnam was winding down. It would be over by the time I re-grouped and figured-out another plan. My personal crusade to salvage the reputation of my fellow veterans was becoming less realistic with every passing hour.

For the next fifteen years I simply avoided mentioning that I was a veteran. My service was not an asset. It was the opposite. Considering the negative attitudes of my fellow citizens, noting that I had served in Vietnam was similar to saying that I had been convicted of a crime and had spent a year in prison.

I was a senior in college, majoring in journalism. The VA did pay for my final two years of college. Time-wise, I was already two years behind everyone else my age. Switching to another curriculum would have put me even further behind. Besides, after all that had happened, my enthusiasm was waning. Rather than give-up, I decided to concentrate on something more practical: advertising. I finally graduated from Wayne State University with a less-than-stellar grade point average. My degree was a Bachelor of Arts in Journalism with a concentration in advertising.

I managed to snare a menial job, in the advertising department, at the suburban *Macomb Daily* newspaper. I parlayed that position into another job, as an advertising representative, at the *Richmond Review* and *St. Clair County Independent Press*, a rural weekly paper. Driving to every small community between Port Huron and New Baltimore, Michigan, selling retail and classified advertising. It was fun.

Jeannie Towar, an advertising rep from the *Macomb Daily*, phoned to say that she had heard about an opening at the *Detroit Free Press*. She gave me the name of the Retail Advertising Manager, and his phone number. She suggested that I use her as a reference. I called, made an appointment for an interview and got the job.

I sold retail advertising for the *Detroit Free Press*, with a figurative vengeance. I liked the work and wanted to heap revenge upon the competing *Detroit News*. It seemed fitting that the best way to pile retribution on the newspaper that fired me was through their pocketbook. I worked tirelessly to decrease the *News'* advertising revenue. I was so effective at selling against my competitor that the Retail Advertising Manager, from the *Detroit News*, sought me out at a party and offered me a job as a manager! Even though it would have meant a sizable pay increase and a title, I turned down his offer.

But the winds of change were gathering in Detroit's newspaper industry. A well-intended piece of legislation titled 'The Newspaper Preservation Act' would result in both of the city's major newspapers being sold. Their new owners used a loophole in the new law to end the competition that had kept both papers strong and vibrant. The newspapers were combined into one amalgamated super-corporation. The newly-formed newspaper conglomerate was guaranteed to make profits into perpetuity. One half of the city's former editorial powerhouse was laid-off. The combination of half the city's watchdogs no longer being on guard, white flight and a series of corrupt political administrations sealed Detroit's fate. It was a crucial moment, Detroit's immanent decline was under-reported by a factor of 50%. An entire city began to auger into a downward spiral. *Detroit's fate was sealed.*

BOB NIEMIC

I couldn't bear to watch the demise of my hometown—I moved from a city beside a river to a city beside a river and a lake…Chicago.

A curious set of circuitous circumstances, involving both the *Sun Times'* and the *Chicago Tribune*'s suburban spin-off newspapers, led to my working for the *Chicago Tribune*. My path, to employment at the *Chicago Tribune* had gone through The *Suburban Trib* a wholly owned subsidiary of the *Chicago Tribune*. The *Suburban Trib* was shut-down. Rather than lay-off dozens of experienced people and effectively send them directly to the competing *Sun-Times*, the *Tribune* incorporated everyone into their staff, we were second-class citizens. The *Chicago Tribune* was nation's fifth largest newspaper. None of the venerable old newspaper's hierarchy knew about my experience in Vietnam, the *Detroit News* or the *Detroit Free Press*. I was good at generating revenue for this newspaper.

However, I was an enigma to the old boy network of supervisors. I never spoke about being a Vietnam Veteran or my editorial experience since these had no bearing on my position as a Retail Advertising Representative. The deteriorating state of Detroit's newspapers was a local situation, relatively unknown in Chicago, and not a positive aspect to highlight on my resume. So, I quietly did my job. My success puzzled my co-workers. I had unintentionally developed some enemies. I didn't even suspect that Bob Niemic believed I was a threat to his career..

Bob had sold retail advertising for over twenty years and occupied a desk close to mine. Bob was a WWII Marine veteran, twenty-five years my senior. Niemic was physically fit, considering his age, and extremely proud of his service. His salt-and-pepper hair was cropped in a military flattop brush style, popular back in the 1950's.

I deliberately didn't share that I was a Vietnam Veteran. Bob seemed like a VFW kind of guy and I didn't need that kind of aggravation. Besides, I'm fairly certain that my service was not even noted on my personnel file. I didn't usually take much time off from work either. So my taking a weekday off, in June of 1986 was unusual. I was going to *Chicago's Welcome Home Parade for Vietnam Veterans*. Twelve years after the war's end, seventeen years after my return, my fellow Americans were displaying some gratitude for our service and sacrifice. I would not have missed that parade for the world.

Niemic hadn't attended the parade, he noticed that I had—even he was able to figure out that I must have been a Vietnam Veteran. I didn't know, or particularly care, about what old Bob thought about Vietnam. I didn't need his permission to attend a parade.

The Parade was *so cool.*

Don Morris, a friend of mine, had been a Marine. Don had guarded the embassy in Saigon, worked in the very same building made infamous by those rooftop evacuation pictures. We went to the parade together. I took pictures. We both drank beer. A good time was had by all.

Back at work, after the parade, I needed a page (tearsheet) from the paper for one of my clients. It was a routine sort-of-thing. Close by, I asked Bob for one of the pages from his paper, after he finished reading the comics. Bob interpreted my innocent comment, about his reading the comics, as some kind of personal insult.

He exploded in a fit of rage. Bob sprang from his seat, grabbed my necktie and pinned me to the file cabinets that lined the office walls. He told me, in front of everyone in the office, that he believed Vietnam Veterans were drug soaked losers and for two cents he would *beat the shit out of me right there on the spot.*

I wasn't in too bad of shape myself and could have easily dropped the old man like a bad habit. Until that moment, I actually liked him. I respected his service. Obviously, he felt no camaraderie for a fellow veteran. I was jammed up against the file cabinets, unsure about my next move. I didn't intentionally provoke the old guy. I didn't want to hurt Bob. I wound-up standing there, taking verbal abuse, until a couple of Bob's friends pulled him off of me. I didn't want to complain to our supervisor or do anything that would imperil his, or my, career. Bob was close to retirement.

At the same time, I didn't want to work with a head-case two desks away.

Therefore I rationalized: I had done good work for the *Tribune*. People with lesser revenue numbers were receiving awards while I had received very little recognition. Niemic's assault was the last straw. I suppose I could have asked for a transfer. But, I was a multi-talented guy and didn't deserve this kind of hassle. It was probably time for me to move on.

I walked into my supervisor's office and tendered my resignation.

WELCOME HOME,
VIETNAM VETERANS!

The Chicago Vietnam Veterans Welcome Home Parade happened on June 13, 1986.

It was a beautiful day. Don Morris, a friend who had been a Marine Guard at the U.S. Embassy in Saigon, attended the festivities with me. We arrived early and joined the veterans forming up on the neglected remains of a derelict Navy Pier. Don and I had not signed-up with any organizations like the American Legion. We had not kept in touch with our old units. For us, there had been no planning or arrangements. Even though we had known that the parade was going to happen for weeks, the event itself was more spontaneous.

Chris Noel

We just 'hung loose' and watched the whole thing develop as the numbers of veterans grew. Don and I had a rough idea of when the parade was supposed to start but we didn't know the route. The whole event was disorderly and refreshingly unmilitary. This was carnival.

Personally, I had come to observe as much as participate. It was an absolutely perfect summer's day as the former GIs funneled off of the Pier and onto the streets of Chicago.

The scale was unexpectedly large. I didn't think that there would be that many veterans or that there would be that many spectators. The people of my adopted hometown turned-out in huge numbers cheering their support, showering us with confetti and gratitude. The warmth of our welcome was amazing and appreciated

The pictures I shot that day reminded me of how much I loved photography. Shortly after the parade, I left the *World's Greatest Newspaper* looking for a better deal.

For me the *Saigon Shuffle* started in Detroit, continued through to 1986. It was an integral part of my personal history. I will always consider myself to have been luckier than most and am proud to have served my country.

The game continues. And, as anyone who has ever dealt with a bureaucracy knows, the *Shuffle* has never stopped. The *Shuffle* has relocated to the Middle East. The participants from our side are all volunteers—**NO MORE DRAFT**. But, now our service men and women endure more deployments and suffer even more emotional stress. The numbers of dead and wounded are carefully managed. Body count has lost its significance. The number of dead civilians has been de-emphasized and trivialized. Whistle-blowers are labeled as traitors and imprisoned.

Spectators are discouraged from viewing the carnage and are only allowed to see very carefully edited glimpses of selected 'newsworthy' segments.

The people running the newest *Shuffle* didn't participate in the *Saigon Shuffle*. But the *Saigon Shuffle* did provide a valuable learning experience for improving the skills required for running an even larger and more expensive con-game.

Don Morris helping paint an improvised sign.

General William Westmoreland

Searching for names on the Vietnam Traveling Memorial Wall

The original *Saigon Shuffle* (self-published in 2006) was inspired by the Library of Congress Veteran's History Project. This is an expanded version of that initial book.

SELECT VIETNAM IMAGES CAN BE FOUND IN THE FOLLOWING PERMANENT COLLECTIONS:

Library of Congress' Veterans' History Project

Washington DC

www.loc.gov/vets/

Richard M. Nixon Memorial Library

Yorba Linda, CA

www.nixonfoundation.org

First Division Museum at Cantigny

Wheaton, IL

www.rrmtf.org/firstdivision/

National Veterans Art Museum

Chicago, IL

www.nvam.org

50401504R00139

Made in the USA
Charleston, SC
23 December 2015